A SEWN

Vintage LIFESTYLE

Verna Mosquera

D&C

David and Charles

Cincinnati, Ohio

Table of Contents

Introduction

I am so excited for the debut of my first book. As I prepare to share my many fabric designs and the projects I've created from them, I realize my life until now has been an incredible journey. It seems only fitting to share more about myself and the path that led me here.

I was born and raised in the San Francisco Bay Area. My parents both immigrated to the United States from Latin America—my mother from Guatemala and my father from Uruguay.

I expressed creative interests early in my childhood. I would spend summers lining up my stuffed animals in my room and drawing portraits of them. My parents tapped into my artistic talents and were quick to place me with a private tutor who taught me the fundamentals of drawing and painting. My grade school teachers would often receive my artwork as gifts at the end of each school year.

My maternal grandmother lived with us on and off during my childhood. It was with her that I was first introduced to sewing and handwork. When I once again showed great interest in working with my hands, my parents enrolled me in a sewing class at the local

mall. The class assignment was to make a vest; I made a three-piece suit, clearly showing signs of the overachiever.

I attended a very structured high school, and in those years, my attention was focused heavily on academic studies. I wasn't able to take an art class until the last semester of my senior year. Creative endeavors were more about the occasional sketch I'd give to a boyfriend or a fun Halloween costume I'd make for a friend.

Having graduated at the young age of sixteen, I decided to stay local for my college studies. I attended the University of California State, Hayward, where, with the help of faculty, I created my own major. I hold a bachelor of arts degree in Marketing the Arts.

Continuing on the education fast track, I completed my studies at the age of twenty. While my marketing classes have been very helpful, my art studies really held my interest. Upon graduating, I went back to take all of the classes I wish I had taken. My studies included Japanese papermaking, printmaking and artist's books. During this time period, I became part of a network of students who would gather on weekends and evenings and just create. I became incredibly passionate about

In my studio, I'm surrounded by things I love: roses, soft hues and treasures. Many of these items inspire my fabric collections.

Vignettes are a part of my creative space. Here are some of my fabrics, bits of my ribbon collection and a delicate needle case made by my dear friend Heidi Gorthy.

my creativity. For the first time, I thought of myself as an artist.

Following in my mothers footsteps and ready to join the workforce, I took a job in real estate sales. I bought a luxury car, nice clothes and my first home by the age of twenty-one. Luckily, I soon realized that material things were not very important to me. Truthfully, I was miserable. After lunch one day, I returned to my office, packed up my desk, quit my job and never looked back.

I decided it was time to travel the world. I sold pretty much everything I owned and moved to my father's homeland, Montevideo, Uruguay. I rented a tiny furnished apartment on the beach. I hand-stitched curtains and pillows, and it became my home for the next eighteen months. Looking back, it was an amazing time of personal growth.

I took classes in serigraphy, pastry making and even importing and exporting—pretty much anything that I could take away from the experience. More than anything else, I spent time getting to know my extended family, spending hours talking with cousins and learning to knit with my aunts on Sunday afternoons. I became deeply aware of the importance of family and all of the amazing opportunities my country had to offer.

During this time, I developed a deep friendship and fell in love with the man who would become my husband, Miguel. He was anxious to travel the world and convinced me to join him on a trip through Europe.

Our adventure started in Paris; we traveled for three months and ended up living in Florence, Italy, for nearly a year. We rented an apartment just across the Ponte Vecchio overlooking the Arno River. Miguel took a job selling leather goods in a tourist shop, and I studied Italian and, of course, art. I was part of an amazing program where a student would spend time with a local artisan in his studio for several hours a week. I studied ceramics, Florentine papermaking and bookbinding. I also spent numerous hours working on embroidery projects. There is no doubt that my love of that which is antique, worn and unique came from wandering those cobblestone streets.

While my time in Florence was amazing, I deeply longed to return to the United States to be with my mom, dad and brother. Miguel and I returned to the San Francisco Bay Area and married a few months later. About a month before we married, I decided to take a quilting class as a New Year's resolution to continue to be creative.

I was hooked on quilting from the very first night. I would spend hours cutting and piecing; I was truly passionate from the word go. I loved the endless fabric selections and plethora of patterns. Not long after this first class, I was asked by the owner to work in the quilt store. It started as one day a week and quickly grew into many more hours. I was also asked to teach a class. The first one I taught had six students. I was very nervous, but I loved it!

Before long, I was teaching several classes a week along with working in the shop. In an effort to become a well-rounded teacher, I took a class in appliqué. It was very difficult for me. I spent fifty hours on my first block and even shed tears of frustration. However, I was determined to learn and finally mastered the technique.

After several years of quilting, I was becoming less interested in working on other people's patterns. Luckily, a designer by the name of Robyn Pandolph was coming to town and teaching an appliqué class. In the first five minutes of class, she asked us to take our pattern and turn it over and draw our own design on the back. I remember looking around the room and seeing how intimidated everyone was. Then I thought to myself, "What am I worried about? I can draw!"

Life has never been the same since. I did not finish the project from the class, nor did I ever work on anyone else's pattern again.

I began working on layout ideas, sketches and color schemes. I also took on the hardest and most fulfilling job I have ever had, that of being a mother and raising my two sons: Milo, eleven, and Nico, eight. Shortly after our second son was born, Miguel and I decided to launch our company, the Vintage Spool. Even though he has always been behind the scenes, Miguel has been tremendously instrumental in our success.

We started with two designs, and by the end of our first year, we had six. By the time we attended our first International Quilt Market, we had twelve pattern designs (currently we sell more than thirty worldwide). It was at that very first market where I met the previous owner of FreeSpirit Fabrics, Donna Wilder. She was enthusiastic about my designs and asked if I would be interested in doing a line of fabric. I explained to her that I was not only a business owner but also a full-time mother to my two young sons. Because of this and the tremendous growth of my company, my first collection of fabric took a while to come to fruition.

FreeSpirit has since been sold and is now a division of Westminster Fibers. I am currently working on

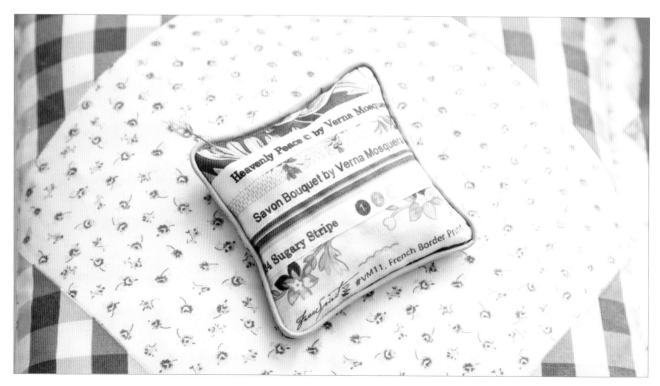

The first time I saw my name on the selvage was pretty special. This darling pincushion was made by a loyal student and friend, Sally Silzars.

My in-home Vintage Spool studio is one of my favorite places. Time spent here is always cherished.

my eighth collection of fabric and now design my Vintage Spool patterns exclusively from my own fabric collections for FreeSpirit. It is wonderful to work on a creative concept from start to finish. The projects in this book are all made exclusively from my fabric collections as well as FreeSpirit Basics.

Along the Vintage Spool journey, my children have been very much a part of my working environment. I often work alongside them as I embark on my creative days. From a very young age, they recognized that quilting and art would be as much a part of their daily lives as it was mine. I try to involve them as much as possible. When they were smaller, they would play with my fat quarters and decorate the studio with them. Now that they are older, I often ask them for creative input, such as what to include in a design or what to name a pattern. They love to come and help at our Vintage Spool workshops.

I feel incredibly blessed to work in a field that I have a tremendous passion for while raising my children at the same time. My days are filled with color, design and constant creativity, all of which I hold dear as an artist. That is not to say that my days are stress free; I do keep many balls in the air most of the time, and occasionally one falls.

While I have worked incredibly hard, my success has not come solely from my own endeavors. It has been a combination of many people working together toward a common goal. I owe so much to all who have helped along the way. I am also incredibly grateful for all those who have embraced my designs, taken my classes and purchased my patterns and fabrics. Thank you for all of your support!

This book is a compilation of all I have learned in my creative journey. The projects I have created include patchwork, appliqué and embroidery that can adorn your home. My hope is that *A Sewn Vintage Lifestyle* will inspire you to create and that your time creating can be as enjoyable for you as it is for me. I am honored to share this book with you.

Verna

Appliqué Supplies and Techniques

My first experience in appliqué was not the greatest. I took a class in needleturn because I was a new quilt instructor and felt it was important to learn many techniques. I realized quickly I was in over my head as I started with a Baltimore Appliqué project. Unbeknownst to me at the time, it was very challenging work for a beginner. Never one to back down from a challenge, I kept working until I finally perfected the technique. That challenge did, however, include many tears and much frustration.

Never in a million years did I think I would specialize in appliqué. It is now my very favorite thing to do. I am so thrilled that many of my students have been inspired enough by my designs to learn to appliqué in order to complete them. The following tools and tips have led me to a much more satisfying appliqué experience.

GENERAL APPLIQUÉ SUPPLIES

For each of the appliqué projects in this book, have the following supplies on hand.

Freezer paper: You'll use freezer paper to transfer the appliqué shapes onto fabric. I use C. Jenkins freezer paper because it comes in different size sheets that are easy to transport. I also like how well it sticks to the fabric, yet it removes easily without leaving any residue.

Black permanent marker: Used for tracing the appliqué shapes, I like the fine line of the Ultra Fine Point Sharpie.

Paper scissors: To cut shapes from freezer paper.

Fabric marking pencil: You'll use the pencil to trace around the template shapes on the fabric. Use a gray fabric pencil for light fabrics and white for dark fabrics. I highly recommend Sewline Fabric Pencils because they always stay sharp and make a nice fine line on the fabric. They do not drag or catch the way other marking tools do.

Fabric scissors: For cutting out large fabric shapes, I prefer the Omnigrid 8½" (21.6cm) fabric scissors.

Small fabric scissors: For clipping the fabric inner curves or deep Vs, I use the Omnigrid 4" (10.2cm) scissors.

Appliqué pins: For pinning the appliqué shape to the background, I recommend using pins made specifically for appliqué. I use Jeana Kimball ¾" (1.9cm) appliqué pins because they are large enough to hold the piece in place but are small enough not to get caught on my thread while stitching.

#10 straw needles: This needle size is ideal for appliqué, and I prefer using the Jeana Kimball brand needle. It threads easily, and the length of the shaft helps to turn under the fabric. The strength of the needle keeps it from bending too much while stitching.

Thread to match your appliqué fabric: A fine, smooth thread works best for appliqué, and I prefer DMC machine embroidery thread. It is very affordable and comes in a wonderful array of colors. It rarely knots up, and if it does, the knot is easy to remove. It is very fine, making it easy to hide my stitches, but strong.

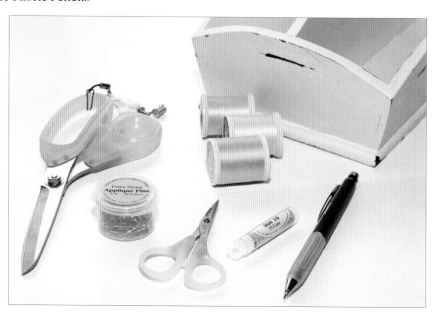

APPLIQUÉ PREPARATION

The following are the steps I use when I prepare the shapes for appliqué. Taking time with the prep can ensure a smoother process and a nice finished product.

1   Trace all appliqué shapes onto the matte side of the freezer paper. Mark portions of the template that will be overlapped by another piece using dotted lines.

2   Number each freezer paper template. Using paper scissors, cut out the freezer paper shapes on the lines.

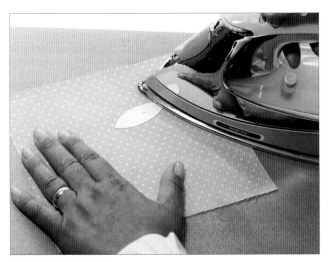

3   Lay the shiny side of the freezer paper onto the right side of the appliqué fabric, and press with a steam iron.

4   Draw around the outside of the freezer paper on the appliqué fabric with a fabric pencil.

5 Cut out the fabric pieces ⅛" (3.2mm) outside of the marked lines.

7 Place the appliqué pieces down one at a time, removing the paper template as you place each piece. Use appliqué pins to secure each piece.

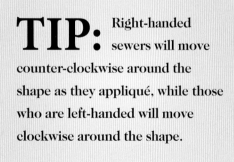

TIP: Right-handed sewers will move counter-clockwise around the shape as they appliqué, while those who are left-handed will move clockwise around the shape.

6 Cut out your background to the designated measurement. If desired, mark placement lines on your background fabric for guidance with the fabric pencil. For a vine, I would draw a single line down the center. For a leaf, I would draw a line indicating the widest point. Just make sure all placement lines fall within the image so they can be easily covered by the fabric shape. You may also eyeball the placement.

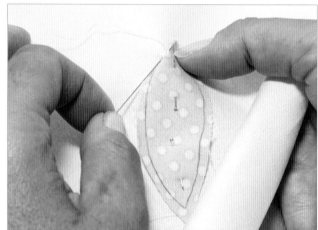

8 Hand-stitch the edges of the appliqué piece using a #10 straw needle, machine embroidery thread and the blind hem stitch. To start this stitch, knot the thread and start the stitching from the underside of the background fabric. Come up through the background and the turned edge of the shape, coming as close to the edge as possible. Continue stitching, turning the edge just past the marked line as you go.

To finish, take the needle to the underside of the background fabric. Take a small bite of fabric with the needle, then knot the thread.

It is not necessary to needleturn the edges of a piece if it will be overlapped by another piece.

POINTS

Nice clean points are essential in appliqué. The steps below are my secrets to success in this area.

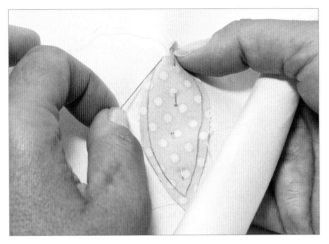

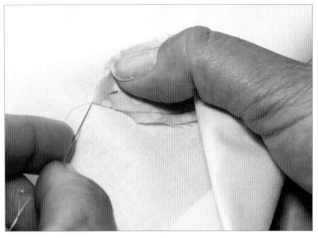

1 To get clean points in your appliqué shape, turn and stitch the allowance on one side; stop stitching just prior to the point. This will cause the allowance from the opposite side to extend out to create a bunny ear. Take one stitch in place prior to the marked turning line to secure the point. Trim the bunny ear.

2 Create a pleat within the seam allowance on the unsewn side. Tuck the bottom part of the pleat under. Then tuck the top part of the pleat under. Take a small stitch in the point. Then continue sewing up the other side of the appliqué shape.

INNER CURVES AND DEEP VS

It's easy to overwork areas that require clipping. Use caution and utilize the side of your needle to avoid frayed fabric in these delicate areas.

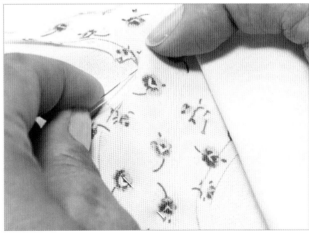

1 When you come to an inner curve or a deep V of an appliqué shape, clip the fabric of the curve or V with your small scissors just beyond the marking line.

2 On the curve or the V, you'll need to stitch in a tiny bit deeper in order to catch the fabric because the fabric around the cut is very delicate. If you come up on the folded edge, it is likely the fabric will fray. So I move that one stitch in so as to catch a bit more fabric.

Embroidery Supplies and Techniques

My mother taught me to cross-stitch when I was in middle school. I'd pick it up and put it down, completing projects here and there. She reinforced how important it was to keep the back of the work looking as lovely as the front, something I still follow to this day.

When I began to design quilt patterns, I realized I would achieve wonderful details in my projects if I knew a few basic embroidery stitches. I am mainly self-taught. As with many other things in my sewing experience, I picked up hints from other sewers and quilters along the way. I am by no means an expert, but I feel I have conquered a few basic stitches that I will share with you here.

GENERAL EMBROIDERY SUPPLIES

For each of the embroidery projects in this book, have the following supplies on hand.

Form-Flex: This is an iron-on stabilizer that I use in embroidery rather than hooping my background fabric. It can be found online or at your local quilt retailer.

Fabric marking pencil: You'll use the pencil to trace the embroidery design onto fabric. Use a gray fabric pencil for light fabrics and white for dark fabrics. I highly recommend Sewline Fabric Pencils because they make very fine lines that are easy to see but also easy to cover with embroidery floss.

Small fabric scissors: For cutting threads, I prefer the Omnigrid 4" (10.2cm) scissors.

#9 embroidery needles: I find the #9 size needle is perfect for all my embroidery needs. My favorite brand is the Jeana Kimball #9 Redwork Embroidery Needle. It has a nice sharp point and is strong, so it does not bend easily. It is also very easy to thread.

Embroidery floss: I am partial to good quality floss so the stitching experience is a pleasant one. Less expensive threads tend to tangle and fray. I use Anchor brand floss.

Stem Stitch/Outline Stitch

I use this stitch for redwork to outline details or embroider words in a project.

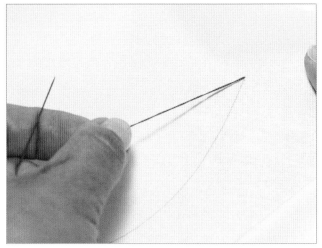

1 Thread the needle with 2 strands of floss (or 1 strand if you're doing very small details) and knot one end. Mark the line to be stitched with the fabric pencil. Bring the needle up through the fabric to the right side of the line to be outlined.

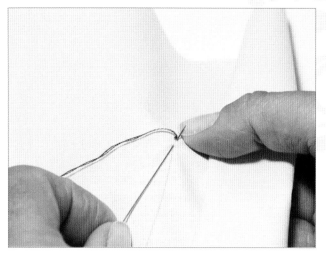

2 Take a short slanting backstitch along the marked line. The needle comes back up where the floss first came out of the fabric. Keep the floss above the needle.

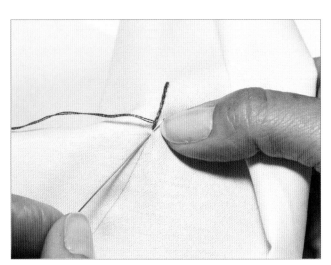

3 Continue taking even stitches with the point of the needle, always coming up where the last stitch went down and keeping the floss above the needle. Keep your stitches small and uniform.

TIP: If you prefer to use a brand of floss other than Anchor, you can find color conversion charts online. One source for converting the Anchor colors to DMC brand colors is stitchtastic.com; the chart is under the "Useful Stuff" category.

Satin Stitch

I use this stitch when I want to fill in a shape such as a leaf or flower petal.

1   Thread 1 strand of floss on the needle and knot
     one end. Mark the line to be stitched with the
     fabric pencil. To start, bring your needle up from
     the back of your fabric along the pattern line.

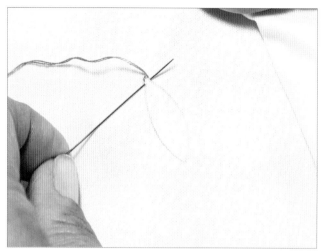

2   Reinsert your needle directly across from your
     last exit point. You'll be making stitches that span
     all the way across the shape.

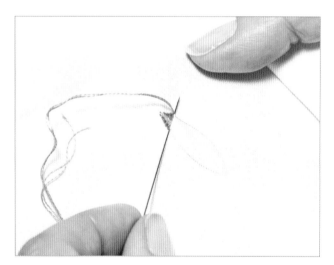

3   Pull the floss all the way through, and you have
     your first stitch in the process. Start your next
     stitch across from the end of your last stitch, and
     the stitch will end right beside the previous stitch.
     The stitches need to be as close to side by side as
     possible. If the stitches aren't close enough, you'll
     have a little gap of fabric peeking through.
          Note that with the satin stitch, the back of your
     fabric will look the same as the front.

FRENCH KNOT

I use this stitch for dotting letters, as small eye accents or in a cluster for flower centers.

1   Thread the needle with 2 strands of floss and knot one end. Mark the dot to be stitched with the fabric pencil. Bring the floss up through the back of the fabric. Hold the floss with one hand and the needle in the other hand. Wrap the floss around the needle 3 times.

2   Put the needle back down into the fabric right next to where the needle came up. Slide the knot down the needle, holding the floss taut. Hold the knot in place under your thumb and push the needle through the fabric.

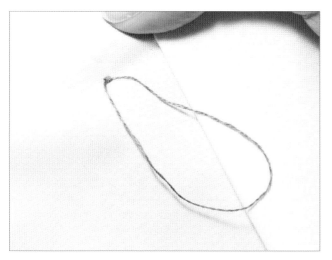

3   Carefully pull the thread through the knot. Go slowly as to not distort the knot.

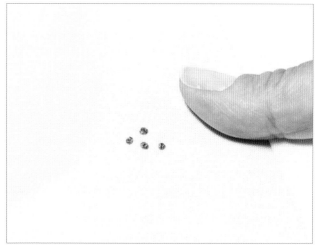

4   Secure the knot in place by catching 1 or 2 strands of thread from the background fabric on the wrong side of the embroidery. Make a loop and take your thread through the loop to create a tiny finishing knot. Secure each knot prior to doing the next French knot. Cut the thread after each knot, rather than travel from one knot to the next, as the thread will show through to the front.

Patchwork Supplies and Techniques

When I was studying Japanese papermaking, I was intrigued by quilt blocks and would use the imagery in my collage work. One day, as a New Year's resolution, I decided to learn to quilt. I chose to do a class in patchwork. My first project was a sampler that included many types of pieced blocks.

It was so important for me to have the correct fundamentals for cutting, piecing and pressing. I still abide by many of those same steps today. In the following steps, I will share a bit about what I've learned along my patchwork path.

GENERAL PATCHWORK SUPPLIES

For each of the patchwork and sewing projects in this book, have the following supplies on hand.

Clear acrylic ruler: You'll use this clear ruler with your rotary cutter and cutting mat to cut the fabric. I prefer the Omnigrid 6" × 12" (15.2cm × 30.5cm) ruler because it is an easy size to hold and the markings are clearly visible.

Rotary cutter: This cutter is designed for use with the acrylic ruler and cutting mat. I use the Olfa ergonomic 45mm rotary cutter because the size makes it easy to maneuver, and it cuts cleanly through four layers of fabric. It is also easy to change the blade and comfortable to use for long periods of time.

Cutting mat: There are many different sizes of cutting mats you can use with your acrylic ruler and rotary cutter. I generally use an 18" × 24" (45.7cm × 61.0cm) cutting mat because I love the size. I can make the majority of patchwork cuts I need, and it transports easily to class.

Thread: Select a neutral-colored thread for your project. For patchwork, I use DMC machine embroidery thread because it's 100% cotton and is multipurpose. I use it for appliqué and bindings, too. It comes in a variety of colors and is fine but strong. I also find it does not leave much lint behind in the bobbin area of my machine.

Straight pins: You'll need pins to hold the fabric pieces together as you sew, and I like Little House straight pins because they are so fine. They insert easily into my fabric and barely leave a mark. They don't cause bulk when pinning intersections, and my sewing machine moves freely over them.

Scissors: For clipping threads, I keep my Omnigrid 4" (10.2cm) scissors handy.

Iron: I feel a high quality iron is extremely important in patchwork. I like a heavy iron and use steam. This combination ensures a great press and, ultimately, more precise patchwork.

Sewing machine: When I started quilting, I made many quilts on an inexpensive sewing machine. Once I realized how much I was enjoying patchwork, I invested in a Bernina. I have never regretted the purchase. The quality of the machine greatly improved my piecing and, quite frankly, made my quilting experience so much more enjoyable. I would highly recommend two features in a machine: needle-down position and a built-in ¼" (6mm) presser foot.

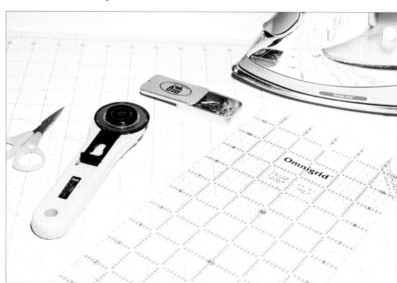

CUTTING

Cut fabric strips along the crosswise grain (from selvage to selvage) because yardage for the quilts is based on crosswise cuts. Most cotton fabrics vary slightly in width from 42" to 45" (106.7cm to 114.3cm). Generally, the crosswise width is assumed to be 45" (114.3cm); it is abbreviated WOF (width of fabric) in the project instructions.

It is important that the crosswise strips be straight. To prevent bent strips, press the fabric first to eliminate any creases. Fold the fabric piece in half widthwise, with the right side facing you and the selvages even with each other. There should no ripples in the fabric. If there are ripples, hold the folded fabric and slide one selvage edge to the right or left until the folded edge is smooth.

You'll be using your acrylic ruler, rotary cutter and cutting mat to cut the fabric shapes. One of the advantages of using the rotary cutter is being able to cut through up to four thicknesses of fabric at a time. However, when working with stripes, plaids or directional prints, the results are better if you cut through only one thickness at a time.

CUTTING STRIPS

When cutting strips, work slowly and accurately. Before you begin, align the folded edge of the fabric along one of the horizontal lines on the cutting mat to ensure straight lines.

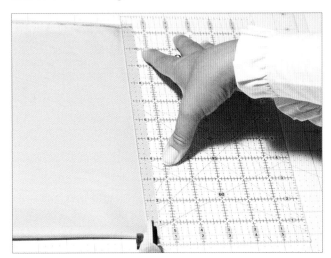

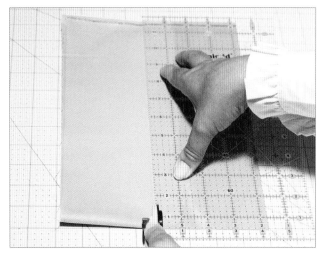

1   Lay your fabric on the cutting mat. If you are cutting multiple layers, first fold the fabric to 4 thicknesses. Then use your ruler and rotary cutter to straighten one edge.

2   Place the marking for the width of the strip even with the newly cut edge of the fabric. Then use the rotary cutter to cut off a strip of fabric.

Continue cutting strips the required width for the pattern you have selected.

Cutting Shapes From Strips

Once strips have been cut, you can use the cutting tools to cut shapes. Use care when moving strips in order to avoid shifting in the cut layers.

Squares

Cut strips the desired width. Then cut the strips apart to make squares. For example, to cut 3" (7.6cm) squares, cut a 3" (7.6cm) wide strip of fabric. Then cut the strip apart every 3" (7.6cm) to make squares.

Rectangles

Cut strips the desired width. Then cut the strips apart to make rectangles. For example, to cut 2" × 4" (5.1cm × 10.2cm) rectangles, cut a 2" (5.1cm) wide strip of fabric. Then cut the strip apart every 4" (10.2cm) to make rectangles.

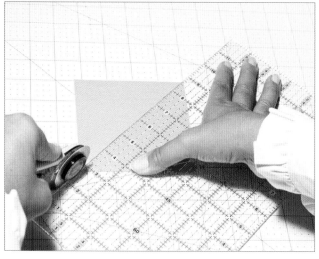

Half-Square Triangles

To cut these triangles, you must know the finished size of side X. Add $7/8$" (2.2cm) to this measurement to determine the size of the strip needed. For example, to cut a triangle with the finished size 3" (7.6cm) on side X, cut a $3\frac{7}{8}$" (9.8cm) wide strip. Cut the strip into $3\frac{7}{8}$" (9.8cm) squares. Then cut the squares in half once diagonally to make triangles. Use caution and cut slowly and accurately because layers can slip on the diagonal cut.

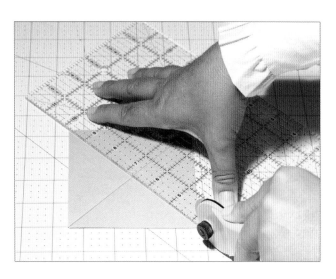

Quarter-Square Triangles

To cut these triangles, you must know the finished size of side X. Add $1\frac{1}{4}$" (3.2cm) to this measurement to determine the size of the strip needed. For example, to cut a triangle with the finished size 3" (7.6cm) on side X, cut a $4\frac{1}{4}$" (10.8cm) wide strip. Cut the strip into $4\frac{1}{4}$" (10.8cm) squares. Then cut the squares into quarters diagonally to make triangles. Use caution and cut slowly and accurately because layers can slip on the diagonal cuts.

PREPARING TO PIECE

Now that individual shapes have been cut, you are ready to begin sewing them into quilt blocks. This is called piecing.

In patchwork, we always use a ¼" (6mm) seam allowance. This is the distance from the cut edge of the fabric to the line of stitching. Unless otherwise indicated, the patchwork projects in this book use a ¼" (6mm) seam allowance.

An accurate ¼" (6mm) seam allowance is crucial to the success of your pieced blocks. It is best to determine the correct placement of the fabric as it travels under the presser foot. Ideally you would have

a ¼" (6mm) presser foot to fit your sewing machine. Take time to learn to make an accurate ¼" (6mm) seam before beginning your patchwork project.

Before you begin sewing, take a few minutes to see that your machine is running smoothly, making even stitches on both the top and the underside. Insert a new needle (80/12 Universal) and remove any lint from the bobbin area of your machine.

Finally, to help prevent errors, organize your workspace and lay out the fabric pieces to be sewn.

PIECING

Piecing should never be rushed. If approached slowly and methodically, it can be very rhythmic and even relaxing!

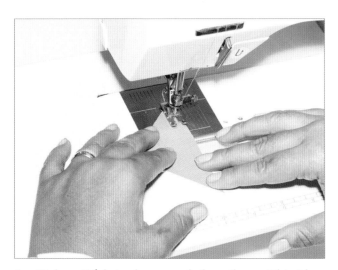

1   Pick up 2 fabric shapes and place them right sides together. Put them under the presser foot and sew them together along the right-hand side. Do not backstitch.

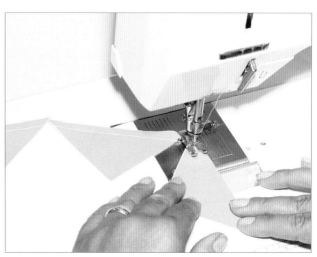

2   To save time, pick up another pair of pieces with right sides together and stitch them right behind the first pair. Do not break the thread. This is called chaining. Continue sewing the remaining shapes together.

PRESSING

Pressing is such an important part of piecing. It is important to press as often as you sew. It can make for much more successful patchwork.

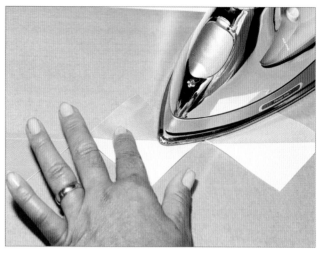

1 Set your steam iron on the cotton setting. Use a padded surface such as an ironing board. With the darker shape facing you, lay the shapes on the ironing board. Press the seam flat on the wrong side. This is referred to as setting the seam.

2 Fold the darker shape back over the stitching line. The seam will be turned in the direction of the darker fabric, preventing it from showing under the lighter fabric.

3 After pressing, clip the threads connecting the shapes. If you're sewing half-square triangles, as I did in this example, trim the extensions to complete the unit.

Strip Piecing

In strip piecing, fabric strips are sewn together in desired combinations. The sewn strips are then cut apart to make new shapes. The width of the cut strips is determined by the individual pattern.

1 Lay 2 strips right sides together and sew along the right side.

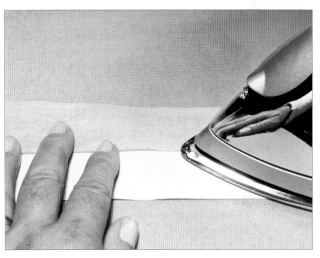

2 Set the seam and press the strips. If needed, sew on any remaining strips. Press.

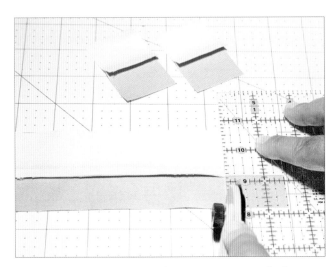

3 Place the strip set on the cutting mat with the wrong side facing up. Cut one short end straight using the rotary cutter and ruler. Then cut pieces as indicated by your quilt pattern.

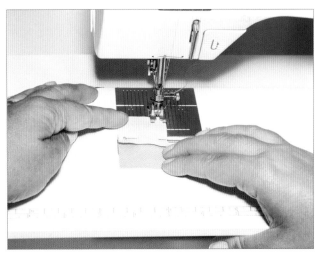

4 You can then take these cut units and join them together, as shown in this Four Patch.

Entertaining and Gathering

What better way to prepare for your guests than to create a few pretty things for your home prior to their arrival? In this chapter, you will learn to make a lovely *Welcome Wall Hanging* for the entry of your home, an adorable *Tablecloth Quilt* for setting tea and a *Patchwork Floor Cushion* and *Lap Quilt* for your friends to rest a spell when they come to visit.

Once your guests arrive, you can prepare delicious treats while wearing your pretty *Flower Apron* and even make doing dishes special by using your delightful *Appliqué Dish Towels* to ease your clean-up.

These projects are perfect for entertaining and gathering.

Appliqué Dish Towels

I'm always on the hunt for fun uses for appliqué. It is a way to add beautiful accents to sewn projects. With these dish towels, you can add a hint of appliqué to charm up the kitchen. The fresh fruit images are so colorful and easy to stitch. It is a great project for someone who is just learning the technique.

SUPPLIES

- ⅝ yard (0.6m) background fabric for each towel
- 1 flour sack for each towel
- Fabric scraps in pinks, greens, yellows, aquas and vintage white for appliqué
- ⅝ yard (0.6m) trim for each towel
- Embroidery floss, Anchor colors #62, #77, #254, #255, #288
- General appliqué supplies, as listed on page 8
- General embroidery supplies, as listed on page 12
- Patterns on pages 128–130

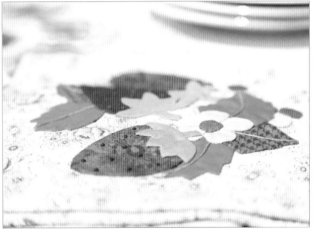

2" (5.1cm)

FIGURE 1

1 Cut a background for each towel
   20" × 28" (50.8cm × 71.1cm).

2 Appliqué the image onto the background
   following the appliqué instructions on pages 9–11
   and using the patterns on pages 128–130. Be
   careful to place the bottom of the image about
   2" (5.1cm) away from the bottom edge of the
   background to leave room for trim (**Figure 1**).

3 After the appliqué is complete, do embroidery
   as indicated on the patterns, following the
   embroidery instructions on pages 13–15. On the
   lemon, use color 255 for leaf veins and 288 for
   the flower centers. On the grapefruit, use 254
   for the leaf veins. On the strawberries, use 254
   for the leaf veins, 77 for the seeds on berries
   1 and 3, and 62 for the seeds on berry 2.

4 Once the appliqué and embroidery
   are complete, trim the background to
   19" × 27" (48.3cm × 68.6cm).

5 Cut a flour sack towel to 19" ×
   27" (48.3cm × 68.6cm).

baste
through
center of
trim

FIGURE 2

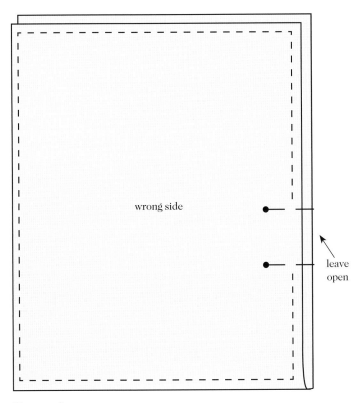

wrong side

leave open

FIGURE 3

6 Baste the trim to the bottom front edge of the background with appliqué (**Figure 2**).

7 Pin and baste the front of the towel with the appliqué to the flour sack with right sides together.

8 Stitch around the outside edge using a ½" (1.3cm) seam allowance, leaving a small gap unstitched on the side edge to allow for turning (**Figure 3**).

9 Press the stitching line.

10 Trim the seam allowance to ¼" (6mm).

11 Turn the towel right side out. Press to ensure a nice clean edge.

12 Whipstitch the opening closed (**Figure 4**).

13 Top stitch around the edge of the towel ¼" (6mm) from the edge.

14 Press the edges of the towel once more to ensure a nice clean finish.

whipstitch opening closed

FIGURE 4

Flower Apron

I'm not sure what it is about the vintage apron that is so fascinating, but I find myself drawn to them. While I must admit I don't spend a great deal of time in the kitchen, wearing a pretty feminine apron does make it sound more appealing. In this design, I decided to combine all the colors in my kitchen along with vintage-inspired elements. The simple construction and attention to detail make this apron wonderfully appealing.

SUPPLIES

- ⅓ yard (0.3m) fabric for ties and mini band (Fabric 1)
- ¾ yard (0.7m) fabric for bib and skirt (Fabric 2)
- ⅓ yard (0.3m) fabric for mini apron band and skirt band (Fabric 3)
- ⅓ yard (0.3m) fabric for mini apron and flower (Fabric 4)
- ¼ yard (0.2m) fabric for ties and flower (Fabric 5)
- 1 yard (0.9m) fabric for lining (Fabric 6)
- 1 covered button, ⅝" (1.6cm)
- Freezer paper
- General patchwork supplies, as listed on page 16
- Pattern on page 122

Cutting Instructions

From Fabric 1:
Cut 2 A neck ties: 2¼" × 31" (5.7cm × 78.7cm)
Cut 2 D side ties: 2½" × 36½" (6.4cm × 92.7cm)
Cut 1 H mini apron band: 4" × 15" (10.2cm × 38.1cm)

From Fabric 2:
Cut 1 B bib: 11" × 12" (27.9cm × 30.5cm)
Cut 1 E skirt: 15" × 44" (38.1cm × 111.8cm)

From Fabric 3:
Cut 1 C waistband: 3" × 21" (7.6cm × 53.3cm)
Cut 1 F skirt band: 5" × WOF (12.7cm × WOF)

From Fabric 4:
Cut 1 G mini apron: 9½" × 15" (24.1cm × 38.1cm)

From Fabric 5:
Cut 2 A neck ties lining: 2¼" × 31" (5.7cm × 78.7cm)
Cut 2 D side ties lining: 2½" × 36 ½" (6.4cm × 92.7cm)

From Fabric 6:
Cut 1 B for bib lining: 11" × 12" (27.9cm × 30.5cm)
Cut 1 C for waistband lining: 3" × 21" (7.6cm × 53.3cm)
Cut 1 E skirt lining: 19" × WOF (48.3cm × WOF)
Cut 1 G mini apron lining: 12½" × 15" (31.8cm × 38.1cm)

Constructing the Apron

1   Place piece A (neck tie) and A lining right sides together. Stitch along the long sides and one end of the tie using a ¼" (6mm) seam allowance. Leave the other end open. Through the open end, turn the tie right-side out and press.

2   Top stitch ⅛" (3mm) in from the edge of the tie along the 3 sewn sides. Leave the remaining end open. Repeat steps 1–2 for the second neck tie.

3   Place 1 neck tie onto piece B (bib), right sides together with the raw edges flush, 1" (2.5cm) from the left edge of the bib. Place the second tie 1" (2.5cm) from the right edge of the bib in the same manner. Baste each tie to the bib (**Figure 1**).

4   Lay the bib lining on the bib with ties (right sides together) and pin. Stitch around the sides and top using a ½" (1.3cm) seam allowance, leaving the bottom of the bib open.

5   Trim the seam to ¼" (6mm). Turn right-side out and press.

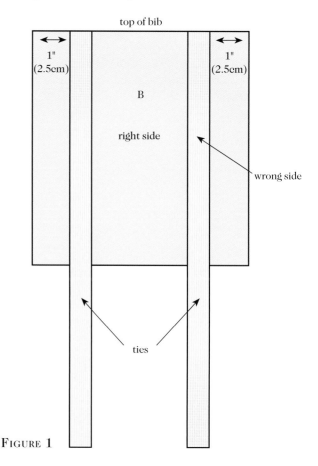

top of bib

1"
(2.5cm)

1"
(2.5cm)

B

right side

wrong side

ties

Figure 1

6   Topstitch ⅛" (3mm) from the edge on the sides and top of the bib, leaving the bottom edge open. Press the stitching line for a clean finish.

7   Pin the bottom edge of piece E (skirt) to the top edge of piece F (skirt band), right sides together. Sew using a ½" (1.3cm) seam allowance. Trim the seam allowance to ⅜" (1cm). Press the seam open.

8   Pin the skirt with the band to the skirt lining, right sides together.

9   Stitch around the side and bottom edges of the skirt using a ½" (1.3cm) seam allowance. Leave the top edge open.

10 Trim the seam to ¼" (6mm). Turn the skirt right-side out and press. Topstitch ⅛" (6mm) from the edges, leaving the top edge open.

11 Run a row of basting stitches ¼" (6mm) from the raw edge along the top of the skirt. Run a second row of basting stitches ⅜" (1cm) from the raw edge along the top of the skirt. Draw in the basting stitches to gather the top edge until the width of the top of the skirt is 20" (50.8cm). Set aside.

12 Pin the bottom edge of piece G (mini apron) to the top edge of piece H (mini apron band), right sides together. Sew using a ½" (1.3cm) seam allowance. Trim the seam allowance to ⅜" (1cm). Press the seam open.

13 Pin the mini apron with the band to the mini apron lining, right sides together. Stitch around the sides and bottom edge using a ½" (1.3cm) seam allowance. Leave the top edge open.

14 Trim the seam to ¼" (6mm). Turn the mini apron right-side out and press. Topstitch ⅛" (3mm) from the side and bottom edges, leaving the top edge open.

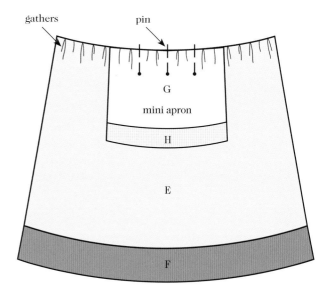

FIGURE 2

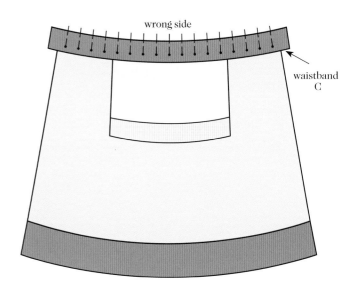

FIGURE 3

15 Find the midpoint of the skirt and the midpoint of the mini apron. Aligning the midpoints, lay the mini apron on top of the skirt, both right sides up. Pin the 2 pieces to hold the mini apron in place (**Figure 2**). Baste the top edge of the mini apron in place.

16 Lay the top edge of piece C (waistband) onto the top edge of the skirt with the mini apron, right sides together. Pin in place. Stitch using a ½" (1.3cm) seam allowance (**Figure 3**).

31

17 Trim to a ⅜" (1cm) seam allowance. Press the seam toward the waistband.

18 Find the midpoint of the top edge of the waistband and the midpoint of the bottom edge of the bib. Align the midpoints, right sides together, and pin. Baste the bib onto the waistband.

19 Lay the top edge of the waistband lining onto the top edge of the skirt with the bib, right sides together. Pin. Stitch the top edge using a ½" (1.3cm) seam allowance (**Figure 4**).

20 Place piece D (side tie) and D lining right sides together. Stitch along the long sides and one end of the tie using a ¼" (6mm) seam allowance. Leave the other end open. Through the open end, turn the tie right-side out and press.

21 Top stitch ⅛" (3mm) in from the edge of the tie along the 3 sewn sides. Leave the remaining end open. Repeat steps 20–21 for the second side tie.

22 Working from the right side of the apron, lay the raw edge of one side tie on the side edge of the waistband, right sides together. Using a ½" (1.3cm) seam allowance, stitch from the top to the bottom edge of the waistband only to attach the side tie (**Figure 5**). Trim the seam to ¼" (6mm). Press the seam toward the waistband. Repeat for the second tie on the opposite side of the waistband.

23 Working from the wrong side of the apron, press under ½" (1.3cm) on all 3 unsewn sides of the waistband lining. Fold the lining over the raw edges of the side ties and waistband. Pin. Hand-stitch the lining in place for a clean finish.

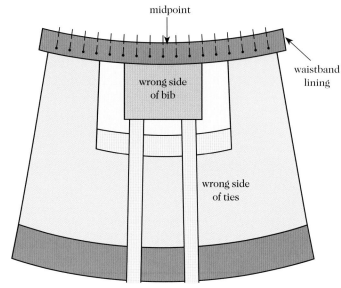

Figure 4

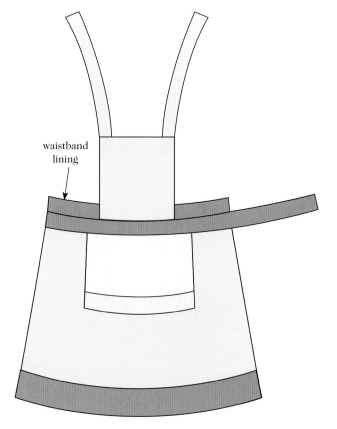

Figure 5

Constructing the Flower

1   Cut 12 freezer paper templates of the flower petal on page 122.

2   From Fabric 4, cut 8 rectangles 3" × 4" (7.6cm × 10.2cm). From Fabric 5, cut 4 rectangles 3" × 4" (7.6cm × 10.2cm).

3   Lay 2 fabric rectangles right sides together. Fuse a freezer paper template to the wrong side of one of the fabric rectangles.

4   With the freezer paper template attached, stitch around the petal shape, leaving the bottom of the petal unsewn (**Figure 6**).

5   Trim around the edge of the stitching line, leaving about ⅛" (3mm) seam allowance.

6   Turn the petal right side out and press. Repeat steps 3–6 for the remaining 11 petals.

7   Turn the open edge of one petal under ¼" (6mm). Topstitch the petal closed. Form a small pleat at the bottom of the petal and stitch it down by machine (**Figure 7**). Repeat for the remaining 11 petals.

8   Join the petals into pairs using a whipstitch (**Figure 8**). You will have 6 pairs.

9   Lay pairs into sets of 4, overlapping the petals perpendicularly. Stitch in place by machine (**Figure 9**).

10 Lay each set of 4 petals on top of each other, rotating each set slightly. All sets should be facing right side up. Stitch all 3 sets in place by hand.

11 Cover the ⅝" (1.6cm) button with the fabric of your choice. Stitch the button to the center of the flower (**Figure 10**).

12 Hand-stitch the flower to the upper portion of the bib, centering it.

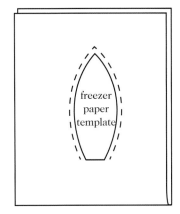
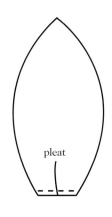

Figure 6   *Figure 7*

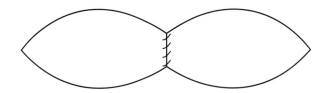

Figure 8

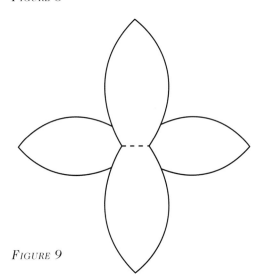

Figure 9

Figure 10

Tablecloth Quilt

This pretty pastel tablecloth quilt is the perfect blend of patchwork and simple appliqué. It serves as the ideal setting for a lovely table of treats. After selecting your favorite fabrics, just create three simple blocks; they are a snap to make. Your family will enjoy this beauty for years to come.

FINISHED SIZE

- 77" × 77" (195.6cm × 195.6cm)

SUPPLIES

- 3¾ yards (3.4m) large floral fabric (Fabric 1)
- ½ yard (0.5m) stripe fabric (Fabric 2)
- 1¼ yards (1.1m) yellow background fabric (Fabric 3)
- ⅝ yard (0.6m) pink polka dot fabric (Fabric 4)
- ⅜ yard (0.4m) aqua check fabric (Fabric 5)
- ⅔ yard (0.6m) aqua polka dot fabric (Fabric 6)
- 1¼ yards (1.1m) pink background fabric (Fabric 7)
- ¼ yard (0.2m) toile fabric (Fabric 8)
- ¾ yard (0.7m) ivory background fabric (Fabric 9)
- ⅔ yards (0.6m) fabric for binding
- 4¾ yards (4.3m) fabric for backing
- General appliqué supplies, as listed on page 8
- General patchwork supplies, as listed on page 16
- Pattern on page 122

Cutting Instructions

From Fabric 1:
Fussy cut 16 A squares centering the flower image: 5" × 5" (12.7cm × 12.7cm)
Cut 4 border strips: 6½" × 88" (16.5cm × 223.5cm)

From Fabric 2:
Cut 32 B squares: 4¼" × 4¼"(10.8cm × 10.8cm), then cut in half on one diagonal

From Fabric 3:
Cut 32 C squares: 5¾" × 5¾" (14.3cm × 14.3cm), then cut in half on one diagonal
Cut 18 J squares: 5¾" × 5¾" (14.3cm × 14.3cm), then cut in half on one diagonal

From Fabric 4:
Cut 12 D squares: 5¾" × 5¾" (14.6cm × 14.6cm), then cut in half on both diagonals
Cut 9 H squares: 5" × 5" (12.7cm × 12.7cm)
Cut 8 border strips: 2" × 45" (5.1cm × 114.3cm)

From Fabric 5:
Cut 12 E squares: 5¾" × 5¾" (14.6cm × 14.6cm), then cut in half on both diagonals

From Fabric 6:
Cut 48 F squares: 4¼" × 4¼" (10.8cm × 10.8cm), then cut in half on one diagonal

From Fabric 7:
Cut 48 G squares: 5¾" × 5¾" (14.3cm × 14.3cm), then cut in half on one diagonal

From Fabric 8:
Cut 18 I squares: 4¼" × 4¼" (10.8cm × 10.8cm), then cut in half on one diagonal

From Fabric 9:
Prep 36 leaves for appliqué using the leaf template provided on page 122.

Making Blocks

Note: The arrows on the diagram indicate which direction to press the seams.

1   Join 1 B triangle to each side of an A square. Press toward the B triangles. Square up all 4 sides of the block, leaving exactly ¼" (6mm) seam allowance before proceeding.

2   Join 1 C triangle to each side of the A/B square. Press toward the C triangles. Square up all 4 sides of the block, leaving exactly ¼" (6mm) seam allowance before proceeding.

3   Repeat steps 1–2 for a total of 16 blocks. These are Block 1 (**Figure 1**).

4   Join 1 D triangle to 1 E triangle. Press toward the E triangle (**Figure 2**).

5   Join 1 D/E unit to another D/E unit (**Figure 3**).

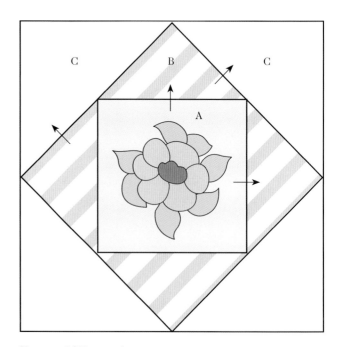

Figure 1/ Block 1

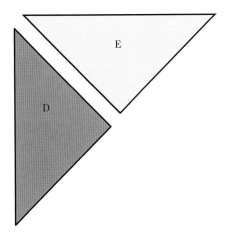

FIGURE 2

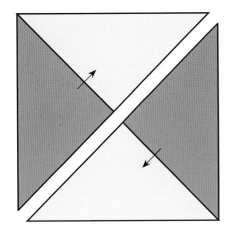

FIGURE 3

06 Join 1 F triangle to each side of the hourglass units. Press toward the F triangles. Square up all 4 sides of the block, leaving exactly ¼" (6mm) seam allowance before proceeding.

7 Join 1 G triangle to each side of the above unit (**Figure 4**). Press toward the G triangles. Square up all 4 sides of the block, leaving exactly ¼" (6mm) seam allowance before proceeding.

8 Repeat steps 4–7 for a total of 24 blocks. These are Block 2.

9 Join 1 I triangle to each side of an H square. Press toward the I triangles. Square up all 4 sides of the block, leaving exactly ¼" (6mm) seam allowance before proceeding.

10 Join 1 J triangle to each side of the H/I square. Press toward the J triangles. Square up all 4 sides of the block, leaving exactly ¼" (6mm) seam allowance before proceeding.

11 Appliqué 4 leaves to the center of the block, following the appliqué instruction on pages 9–11 (**Figure 5**).

12 Repeat steps 9–11 for a total of 9 blocks. This is Block 3.

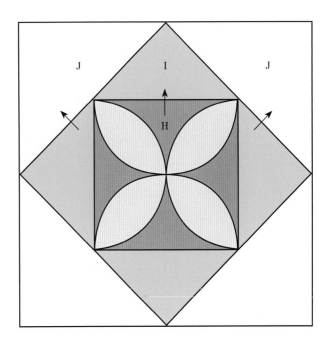

FIGURE 4/ BLOCK 2

FIGURE 5/ BLOCK 3

JOINING BLOCKS AND ROWS

1 For Rows 1, 3, 5 and 7, join 4 of Block 1
   and 3 of Block 2, alternating every other
   block (**Figure 6**). Press toward Block 2.

2 For Rows 2, 4 and 6, join 4 of Block
   2 and 3 of Block 3, alternating every
   other block. Press toward Block 2.

3 Join Rows 1 and 2. Press seam toward Row 2.

4 Continue adding rows 3–7 until all rows have
   been joined together. Press all seams down.

ADDING BORDERS AND FINISHING

1 Join 2 Fabric 4 border strips together on the
   diagonal on the 2" (5.1cm) side. To do this
   place 2 strips together at right angles, with
   right sides together. Draw a line from the top
   corner of the top strip to the bottom corner
   of the bottom strip. It is important to draw
   the line in this manner. Sew on the drawn
   line. Trim the excess fabric from the seam,
   leaving a ¼" (6mm) seam allowance.

2 Repeat 3 additional times for a total of 4 strips.
   One long strip is needed for each side of the quilt.

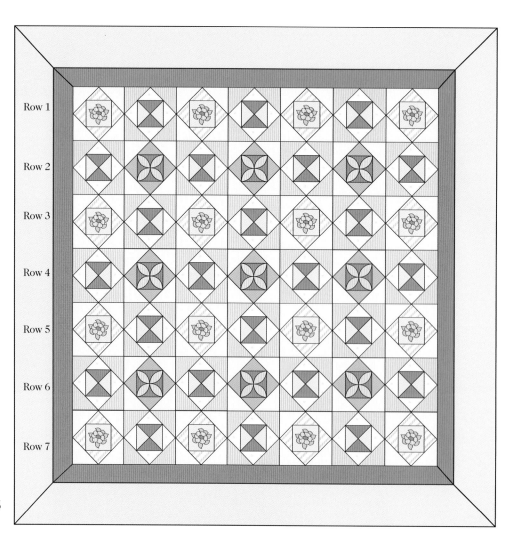

Figure 6

38

3   Find the midpoint of a Fabric 4 border strip and the midpoint of a Fabric 1 border strip, and pin together along the longest side. Join together using a ¼" (6mm) seam. Press the seam toward the Fabric 4 border strip. Repeat 3 additional times for the 3 remaining borders.

4   Find the midpoint of the quilt and the midpoint of the border strip, and pin together with the Fabric 4 strip next to the quilt. Sew, starting

and stopping ¼" (6mm) from each edge. Press the seam toward the border. Repeat 3 additional times for the 3 remaining borders.

5   Miter each corner of the quilt at a 45° angle (see pages 52-53 for instructions). Press the seams open and trim to ¼" (6mm) seam allowance.

6   The quilt top is complete. Layer, baste, quilt and bind as desired.

Patchwork Lap Quilt

This very simple yet playful scrap quilt is so much fun to make. The quaint patchwork block uses several fabric combinations. Choose four color families (I used light pink, dark pink, ivory and green), and mix and match your scraps to create twenty different blocks. Set with sashing, the blocks just pop! This quilt is the perfect throw for any living room and looks lovely over your favorite chair.

FINISHED SIZE

- 54" × 64½" (137.2cm × 163.8cm)

SUPPLIES

- ⅛ yard (0.1m) or one 2½" (6.4cm) strip each of 22 assorted fabrics.
- 3¼ yards (3.0m) neutral or solid ivory fabric
- ½ yard (0.5m) fabric for binding
- 3½ yards (3.2m) fabric for backing
- General patchwork supplies, as listed on page 16

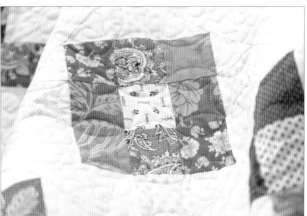

Cutting Instructions

Cut 16 A squares from each of the 22 different fabrics: 2½" × 2½" (6.4cm × 6.4cm). You will have a total of 352 A squares. You will use 260 squares for the blocks and 70 squares for the pieced border; 22 squares will remain to use in another project.

From Neutral Fabric:

Cut 40 B squares for the blocks: 4¼" × 4¼" (10.8cm × 10.8cm), then cut in half on both diagonals, yielding 160 B triangles

Cut 40 C squares for the blocks: 2½" × 2½" (6.4cm × 6.4cm), then cut in half on one diagonal, yielding 80 C triangles

Cut 8 D squares for the pieced border: 2½" × 2½" (6.4cm × 6.4cm), then cut in half on one diagonal, yielding 16 D triangles

Cut 33 E squares for the pieced border: 4¼" × 4¼" (10.8cm × 10.8cm), then cut in half on both diagonals, yielding 132 E triangles

Cut 25 F strips for the sashing: 2½" × 9" (6.4cm × 22.9cm)

Cut 6 G strips for sashing: 2½" × exactly 45" (6.4cm × 114.3cm)

Cut 8 H strips for the plain border: 2½" × WOF (6.4cm × WOF)

Making 20 Blocks

Note: Refer to Figure 1 for color placement as well as for which direction each triangle should face. The arrows on the diagram indicate which direction to press the seams. You can change the position of each color family on every block to add interest to your quilt.

1   For Row 1, join 1 B triangle to each side of 1 A square. Press the seams to the right.

2   For Row 2, join 3 A squares and 1 B triangle to each side of the A squares. Press the seams to the left.

3   For Row 3, join 5 A squares. Press the seams to the right.

4   For Row 4, join 3 A squares and 1 B triangle to each side of the A squares. Press the seams to the left.

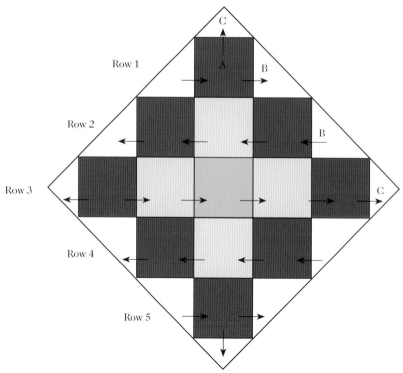

Figure 1

5   For Row 5, join 1 B triangle to each side of
    1 A square. Press the seams to the right.

6   Join Row 1 to Row 2. Press the
    seam toward Row 2.

7   Join Row 3 to Rows 1 and 2. Press
    the seam toward Row 3.

8   Join Row 4 to Rows 1, 2 and 3.
    Press the seam toward Row 4.

9   Join Row 5 to Rows 1, 2, 3 and 4.
    Press the seam toward Row 5.

10 Join a C triangle to each corner of the block.
    Press the seams toward C triangles.

11 Square up around all 4 sides of the block
    leaving ¼" (6mm) from the points out.
    Repeat steps 1–11 for a total of 20 blocks.

JOINING BLOCKS

1   Join 5 short sashing strips (F) with 4
    blocks in between (**Figure 2**). Press
    the seams toward the sashing.

2   Repeat step 1 for 4 additional
    rows, for a total of 5 rows.

3   Join the rows together with long sashing strips
    (G) in between as well as a long sashing strip
    at the top of the rows and one at the bottom of
    the rows. Press the seams toward the sashing.

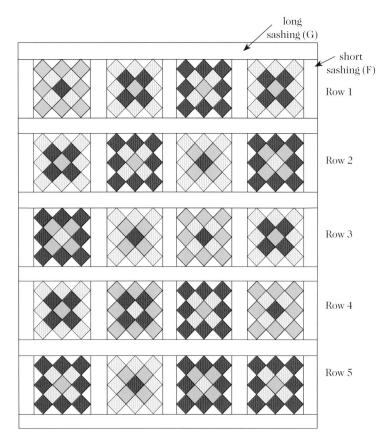

FIGURE 2

MAKING THE PIECED BORDER

1   To create an end unit, join an E triangle to
    an A square. Press toward the E triangle.

2   Join 2 D triangles to the two open sides of the A
    square. Press toward the D triangles (**Figure 3**).

3   Repeat steps 1–2 for 7 more end units
    for a total of 8 end units. Set aside.

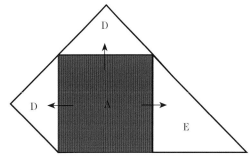

FIGURE 3

4   To make the pieced border units, join an E triangle to each side of an A square (**Figure 4**). Press the seam toward the E triangles. Make 62 of these units.

5   Join 17 of these units, then add an end unit to each end of the pieced border strip. This will create the right-side pieced border.

6   Repeat step 5 for 1 additional border to create the left-side pieced border.

7   Join 16 of these units, then add an end unit to each end of the pieced border strip. This will create the top pieced border.

8   Repeat step 7 for 1 additional border to create the bottom pieced border.

9   Pin the right-side pieced border to the right side of the quilt. Ease to fit because the pieced border is likely to pull in and may appear not to fit at first. Sew. Press the seam toward the sashing.

10   Repeat step 9 for the left-side pieced border.

11   Pin the top pieced border to the top of the quilt. Ease to fit because the pieced border is likely to pull in and may appear not to fit at first. Sew. Press toward the sashing.

12   Repeat step 11 for the bottom pieced border.

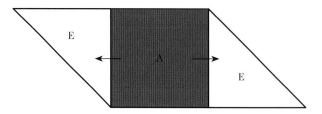

FIGURE 4

ADDING THE NEUTRAL BORDER AND FINISHING

1   Join 2 H strips on the diagonal. Press the seam in one direction and trim to ¼" (6mm) seam allowance.

2   Repeat step 1 to create 3 additional strips, 1 for each side of the quilt.

3   Measure the quilt through the middle from top to bottom. Trim two strips to this measurement. Pin each border to the right and left side of the quilt. Sew. Press the seams toward the border.

4   Measure the quilt through the middle from side to side. Trim two strips to this measurement. Pin each border to the top and bottom of the quilt. Sew. Press the seams toward the border.

5   The quilt top is complete. Layer, quilt and bind as desired.

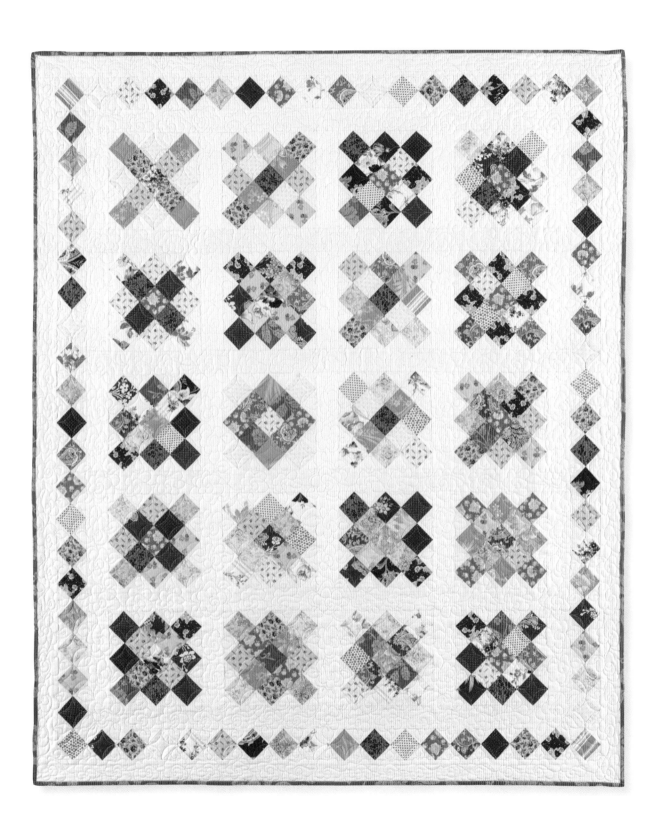

Patchwork Floor Cushion

This fun patchwork cushion adds playfulness to any living room. The mix-and-match fabric combinations are endless. Adding the ruffle brings the romance. You will want to make more than one of this comfy cushion.

FINISHED SIZE

- 22" × 22" (55.9cm × 55.9cm)

SUPPLIES

- ⅝ yard (0.6m) each of two fabrics for patchwork (Fabrics 1 and 2)

- ⅞ yard (0.8m) fabric for sides of cushion (Fabric 3)

- 2⅛ yards (1.9m) fabric for ruffle (Fabric 4)

- ⅜ yard (0.3m) fabric to cover buttons (Fabric 5)

- Embroidery floss, 1 skein neutral

- 18 covered buttons, 1⅛" (2.9cm) each

- 22" × 22" (55.9cm × 55.9cm) cushion form

- 12-ounce bag fiberfill

- 5" (12.7cm) doll needle

- General patchwork supplies, as listed on page 16

Cutting Instructions

From Fabric 1:
Cut 16 A squares for patchwork: 6½" × 6½" (16.5cm × 16.5cm)

From Fabric 2:
Cut 16 B squares for patchwork: 6½" × 6½" (16.5cm × 16.5cm)

From Fabric 3:
Cut 3 C strips for cushion sides: 23" × 5" (58.4cm × 12.7cm)
Cut one D strip: 23" × 3½" (58.4cm × 8.9cm)
Cut one E strip: 23" × 5½" (58.4cm × 14.0cm)

From Fabric 4:
Cut 12 F strips for ruffle: 6" × WOF (15.2cm × WOF)

Making the Patchwork

1   Join A and B squares into rows, alternating 1 A square and 1 B square. Press the seams toward the B squares. Make 8 rows, each with 2 A squares and 2 B squares (**Figure 1**).

2   Join 2 rows together, inverting row 2 so it starts with a B square. Press seam down toward row 2. Make 4 of these (**Figure 2**).

3   Join 2 of above units to create the pillow front. Press the seam toward the bottom unit. Repeat for the pillow back (see **Figure 3**).

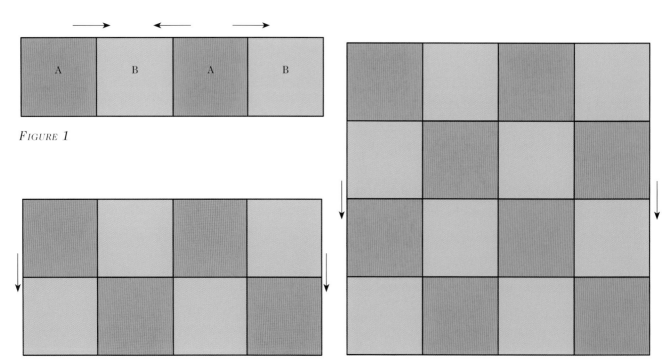

Figure 1

Figure 2

Figure 3

Adding Buttons

1. Following the directions on the button package, cover 18 buttons. Stitch a button onto each patchwork intersection for both the front and back of the pillow.

Making the Ruffle

1. Join 1 ruffle strip to another ruffle strip on the diagonal. Trim the seam to ¼" (6mm) and press open. Repeat until you have joined 6 ruffle strips.

2. Turn under ¼" (6mm) and then another ¼" (6mm) on each short end of the strip. Stitch a hem on each end. Press the strip in half width-wise. This will be the top ruffle.

3. Repeat steps 1–2 for the remaining 6 ruffle strips. This will be the bottom ruffle.

4. Stitch a row of stitching ¼" (6mm) away from the raw edges of the top ruffle strip. Stitch another row of stitching ⅜" (1cm) away from the raw edges of the ruffle. Gather the rows of stitching until the ruffle fits around the sides of the pillow front. Pin the ruffle to the pillow top. Hand-baste the ruffle onto the front of the pillow front.

5. Repeat step 4 for the second ruffle. Pin the ruffle to the pillow back. Hand-baste the ruffle to the front of the pillow back.

Adding Pillow Sides and Finishing

1. Create an opening in the pillow. On side piece D, turn under ½" (1.3cm), then another ½" (1.3cm) along the longest side. Press, then stitch the hem close to fold.

2. On side piece E, turn under ½" (1.3cm), then another ½" (1.3cm) along the longest side. Press, then stitch the hem close to fold.

3. With right sides up, place hemmed edge of E over hemmed edge of D. E will overlap D 2" (5.1cm). Pin, then baste along the hem line.

4. Trim the width of the overlapped strips to 5" (12.7cm).

5. Join the 3 C strips together along the 5" (12.7cm) sides. Press the seams open. Join each side of the D/E piece to one of the C strips, right sides together. This creates a ring.

6. With right sides together, pin the ring to the pillow front on top of the basted ruffle, placing the D/E opening on one side. Line up the seams of the side ring to the corners of the pillow front, pinning a little at a time. Stitch using a ½" (1.3cm) seam allowance and pivoting at each corner. It is quite thick, so you may engage a walking foot on your sewing machine or enlarge your stitch length a bit. After stitching, check to ensure there are no tucks in the seam.

7. Once the seam looks good, press and trim the seam allowance to ¼" (6mm).

8. Repeat steps 6–7 to attach the side ring to the pillow back.

9. Remove the basting stitches from the pillow opening.

10. Insert the pillow form. Press the patchwork squares to remove any wrinkles.

11. Using fiberfill, stuff each side a bit so the pillow fills the cover snugly. Do not stuff the side with the opening. The pillow may require a bit of fiberfill in the corners, too.

12. Using a doll needle and 6 strands of floss, insert the needle at 1 button through the top of the pillow, down through the pillow form and back up through the form. Shift the button momentarily and try to insert the needle and come up as close to the patchwork intersection as possible.

13. Unthread the needle and take the 2 ends of the thread and pull them taut, cinching in at the patchwork intersection. Tie the ends into a knot. Trim the thread and set the button back into place. Repeat for the remaining 8 buttons.

14. On the side of the pillow with the opening, pin the overlap in place to close the opening. Then whipstitch the opening closed and remove the pins.

Welcome Wall Hanging

What better way to welcome guests into your home than with this charming rose-filled wall hanging? This is the perfect project for someone who wants to try hand appliqué. The simple size makes this a wonderful place to start and a lovely gift when finished.

FINISHED SIZE

- 21" × 27" (53.3cm × 68.6cm)

SUPPLIES

- Fat quarter (18" × 22"/ 45.7cm × 55.9cm) of 2 neutral background fabrics (Fabrics 1 and 2)

- Fat eighths (9" × 22"/ 22.9cm × 55.9cm) of 6 assorted shades of pink fabric for roses

- Fat eighths (9" × 22"/ 22.9cm × 55.9cm) of 3 assorted greens fabric for leaves

- Fat quarter (18" × 22"/ 45.7cm × 55.9cm) of green stripe fabric for vine

- ¼ yard (0.2m) fabric for inner border (Fabric 3)

- ½ yard (0.5m) fabric for outer border, or 1 yard (0.9m) if horizontal stripe is used (Fabric 4)

- ⅔ yard (0.6m) fabric for backing

- ¼ yard (0.2) fabric for binding

- Cotton batting (24" × 30"/ 61.0cm × 76.2cm)

- Embroidery floss, Anchor color #77

- General appliqué supplies, as listed on page 8

- General embroidery supplies, as listed on page 12

- General patchwork supplies, as listed on page 16

- Pattern on pages 124–125

CUTTING INSTRUCTIONS

From Fabric 1:
Cut 1 piece for upper background: 13½" × 13½" (34.3cm × 34.3cm)

From Fabric 2:
Cut 1 piece for lower background: 13½" × 7½" (34.3cm × 19.1cm)

From Fabric 3:
Cut 4 strips for inner border: 1" × 32" (2.5cm × 81.3cm)

From Fabric 4:
Cut 4 strips for outer border: 4½" × 32" (11.4cm × 81.3cm)

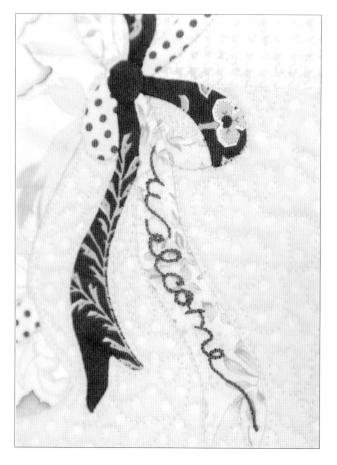

Note: Use ¼" (6mm) seams unless otherwise noted.

1. Join the upper background to the lower background along the 13½" (34.3cm) side. Press the seam toward the lower background.

2. Appliqué the vase with flowers following the general appliqué instructions given on pages 9–11 and using the pattern on pages 124–125.

3. Once the appliqué is complete, embroider the word *Welcome* on the ribbon using the stem stitch and 2 strands of floss. Refer to the embroidery instructions on page 13 as needed.

4. With the appliqué and embroidery complete, press the appliqué from the wrong side. Trim the appliqué background to 12½" × 18½" (31.8cm × 47cm).

5. Join the inner border strip to the outer border strip along the longest side. Press the seam toward the inner border. Repeat for the remaining 3 border strips.

CUTTING FOR MITERED BORDER

Note: When more than one border is used, match the center points of the borders to each other. Sew together lengthwise in one unit before cutting. Treat this unit as one border strip and use the technique described here.

1. Start with Sides A, the left and right sides. Measure from the top to the bottom of quilt through the center. This is measurement A.

2. Measure the width of the border, and multiply this by 2. In this case, your border width is 5" (12.7cm); so your measurement is 10" (25.4cm).

3. Add 2" (5.1cm) to this amount for your working allowance.

4. Total the measurements in steps 1, 2 and 3. For Sides A, you need to cut 2 strips (one for the left, one for the right) to this length.

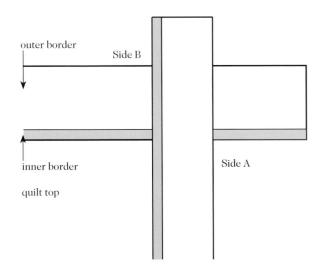

outer border

Side B

inner border

quilt top

Side A

Figure 1

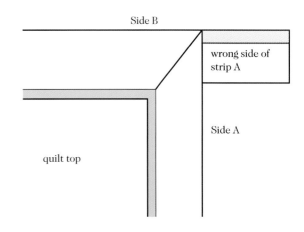

Side B

wrong side of strip A

quilt top

Side A

Figure 2

5   Cut the borders for Sides B, the top and bottom of the quilt. Measure from left to right through the center of the quilt. This is measurement B.

6   Measure the width of the border, and multiply this by 2. In this case, your border width is 5" (12.7cm); so your measurement is 10" (25.4cm).

7   Add 9" (22.9cm) to this amount for your working allowance.

8   Total the measurements from steps 5, 6 and 7. For Sides B, you need to cut 2 strips (one for the top, one for the bottom) to this length.

ATTACHING MITERED BORDER

1   Lay the Side A border strips on each side of the quilt top, right sides together. Find the midpoint of the border and the midpoint of quilt top, and pin. Continue pinning border to quilt top.

2   Beginning and ending ¼" (6mm) from each corner, stitch the Side A borders to the quilt top, with the border strip on top. There will be a generous amount of border fabric extending beyond the quilt top. This is needed to miter the corners. *Do not cut off the excess fabric.*

3   Repeat steps 1 and 2 for both Side B border strips. Remember to start and stop ¼" (6mm) from each corner.

4   Take the quilt top to your pressing surface. Working one corner of the quilt at a time, extend the unsewn border ends out straight, overlapping the end of A over the end of B (**Figure 1**).

5   Lift up the A border strip and fold it under only itself, at a 45° angle. The remainder of border A should lay even with both sides of the underlying B border (**Figure 2**). Press to set the angle.

6   Turn the quilt to the wrong side and place pins near the pressed fold in the corner to hold the border strips in place.

7   With wrong side up, stitch along the folded line in the corner. Be careful to stitch right up to the previous stitching lines in the corner of the quilt line to avoid gaps.

8   Trim excess fabric from the border to ¼" (6mm) seam allowance. Press on the right side.

9   Repeat steps 4–8 for the remaining three corners.

10 Layer, baste, quilt and bind as desired.

Refreshing and Rejuvenating

What better way to make household chores something to look forward to than to surround yourself with pretty, sewn treasures? Beautiful things you create yourself will help to make these daily tasks brighter.

In this chapter, you will learn to make an adorable *Vintage Clothespin Holder*, a charming *Laundry Bag*, and a framed embroidery piece to freshen up your laundry room. Then, once your laundry is complete, make a dainty *Purse Sachet* to keep clothes smelling wonderful, and rejuvenate yourself with a shower behind the pretty *Fabric Shower Curtain*.

These projects and more are just what you need to refresh and rejuvenate.

Vintage Clothespin Holder

What better way to decorate your laundry room than with this darling vintage-inspired clothespin holder? Both functional and charming, this project features the cutest dress shape. Find a child's hanger and your favorite fabric, and away you go. You will have so much fun that you'll want to make them as gifts for all of your friends.

SUPPLIES

- ½ yard (0.5m) fabric for dress (Fabric 1)
- Fat quarter (18" × 22"/ 45.7cm × 55.9cm) fabric for pocket and button cover (Fabric 2)
- Fat quarter (18" × 22"/ 45.7cm × 55.9cm) fabric for pocket lining and neck facing (Fabric 3)
- 2½" × 9½" (6.4cm × 24.1cm) scrap for pocket trim (Fabric 4)
- Child's hanger
- Covered button, ⅝" (1.6cm)
- 3 small millinery flowers
- Freezer paper
- General patchwork supplies, as listed on page 16
- Pattern on page 132

Cutting Instructions

From Fabric 2:
Cut 1 square for pocket: 12" × 12" (30.5cm × 30.5cm)
Cut 1 square for button cover: 2" × 2" (5.1cm × 5.1cm)

From Fabric 3:
Cut 1 square for pocket lining: 15" × 15" (38.1cm × 38.1cm)
Cut 2 rectangles for neck facing: 3" × 6" (7.6cm × 15.2cm)

From Fabric 4:
Cut 1 strip for pocket trim: 1¾" × 8¼" (4.5cm × 21.0cm)

1 Trace the dress pattern onto the matte side of the freezer paper. Cut the freezer paper template out on the line.

2 Fold Fabric 1 in half, right sides together. Iron the freezer paper, shiny side down, onto the wrong side of the dress fabric. Place a few pins around the outside edge of the dress template to hold the 2 layers of fabric together.

3 Cut out 2 dresses, one for the front and one for the back.

4 Trace the pocket pattern onto the matte side of the freezer paper. Cut the freezer paper template out on the line. Iron the freezer paper, shiny side down, onto the wrong side of the pocket fabric.

5 Lay the pocket and pocket trim right sides together, aligning the top edges of the pocket and trim. Stitch using a ½" (1.3cm) seam allowance (**Figure 1**). Press the seam toward the pocket trim. Trim the seam to ¼" (6mm).

6 Lay the pocket with trim onto the pocket lining fabric, right sides together, and pin. Cut out one lining to match the size of the pocket with trim.

7 Sew the pocket and lining together leaving a 2" (5.1cm) opening unsewn at the bottom edge of the pocket.

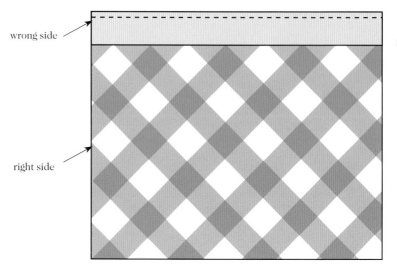

wrong side

right side

fold

FIGURE 1

8 Trim the seam allowance to ¼" (6mm), clipping corners at an angle. Turn the pocket right-side out and press. Whipstitch the bottom opening closed.

9 Using the guideline on the pattern, place the pocket, lining side down, onto the right side of the dress front. Topstitch the sides and bottom of pocket onto the dress front (**Figure 2**).

10 Trace the neck facing pattern onto the matte side of the freezer paper. Cut the template on the line.

11 Lay 2 pieces of neck facing fabric right sides together; fold in half. Cut out 2 neck facing pieces.

12 Lay 1 neck facing onto the dress front, aligning along the top edge of the neck. Pin. Stitch using a ½" (1.3cm) seam allowance. Clip into the curved part of the neckline, taking care not to clip the stitching line (**Figure 3**). Trim the seam to ¼" (6mm).

13 Fold the facing over to the wrong side of the dress front. Press. Turn to the right side of the dress front and top stitch ⅛" (3mm) along the top edge of the neckline.

14 Repeat steps 12–13 for the dress back and its neck facing.

15 Lay the dress front and dress back right sides together. Pin. Stitch using a ½" (1.3cm) seam allowance. Leave an 8" (20.3cm) opening unsewn at the bottom edge of the dress to insert the hanger.

16 Trim the seam to ¼" (6mm). Clip the corners at an angle. Make clips under the arms, using caution not to clip the stitching.

17 Turn the dress right-side out. Press.

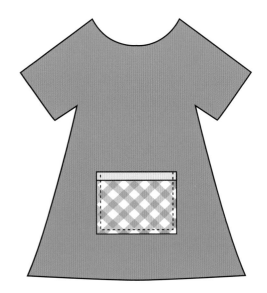

FIGURE 2

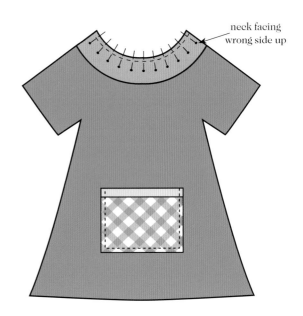

neck facing
wrong side up

FIGURE 3

18 Layer 3 millinery flowers together and stitch the layers together by hand or by machine. Only a few stitches in the center of the flowers are needed.

19 Cover the button with fabric, following the manufacturer's instructions. Stitch the button to the center of the flowers.

20 Stitch the flower embellishment to the top of the dress just under the neckline.

21 Carefully insert the child's hanger. Whipstitch the bottom edge closed.

Laundry Bag

When I looked at my fixer-upper home for the first time, the laundry room was the first place that drew me in. My husband thought I was crazy, but I had a vision of how cute it could be. These laundry bags are the perfect way to add a little romance to an everyday chore. They are not only functional, but their pretty fabrics also help to freshen up the room.

SUPPLIES

- ⅔ yard (0.6m) of 2 different fabrics for laundry bag (Fabrics 1 and 2)
- Scrap fabric for embroidered label, at least 12" × 6" (30.5cm × 15.2cm) (Fabric 3)
- 1¼ yards (1.1m) fabric for lining, casing and tie (Fabric 4)
- Scrap Form-Flex to back label, 8½" × 3¾" (21.6cm × 9.5cm)
- Embroidery floss, Anchor color #1037
- Appliqué thread to match laundry label
- General embroidery supplies, as listed on page 12
- General patchwork supplies, as listed on page 16
- Pattern on page 129

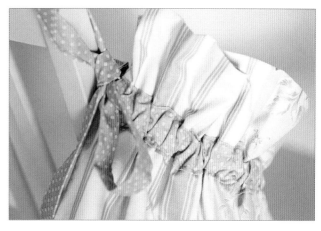

Cutting Instructions

From Fabric 1:
Cut 2 A panels: 11" × 27" (27.9cm × 68.6cm)

From Fabric 2:
Cut 2 B panels 11" × 27" (27.9cm × 68.6cm)

From Fabric 3:
Cut 1 C for embroidered label: 12" × 6" (30.5m × 15.2cm)

From Fabric 4:
Cut 2 D pieces for lining: 21" × 27" (53.3cm × 68.6cm)

Cut 1 E, casing strip: 40½" × 3" (102.9cm × 7.6cm)

Cut 2 F strips for tie: 36" × 4" (91.4cm × 10.2cm)

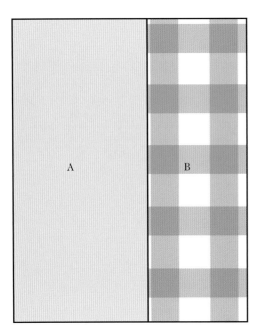

Figure 1

1   Transfer the word *Laundry* from page 129 onto label piece C. Follow the embroidery instructions on page 13 to do the embroidery, using the stem stitch and 3 strands of floss.

2   After completing the embroidery, trim the label to 8½" × 3¾" (21.6cm × 9.5cm).

3   With rights sides together, lay the embroidery piece and the Form-Flex together and stitch, using a ¼" (6mm) seam allowance.

4   Cut a small slit in the center of the Form-Flex, using care not to cut into the embroidered label. Turn the piece right-side out and press.

5   Using a ½" (1.3cm) seam allowance, join 1 A panel to 1 B panel along one long side (**Figure 1**). Press the seam open. Repeat for the second A and B panels.

6   Find the midpoint of the laundry label and align it with the center seam on one A/B panel. The top edge of the label should sit 15½" (39.4cm) from the top edge of the A/B panel (**Figure 2**). Hand-stitch the label to the bag.

7   Pin the laundry bag front to the back, right sides together, aligning each A fabric with the B fabric on the other piece. Sew along the 2 sides and the bottom with a ½" (1.3cm) seam allowance, leaving the top edge open. Clip the bottom corners at an angle, being careful not to clip the stitches. Press the seams open. Turn right-side out.

8   Pin the lining front to the lining back, right sides together. Sew along the 2 sides and the bottom using a ½" (1.3cm) seam allowance. Leave the top edge open, and leave a 3" (7.6cm) opening on the right side of the lining for turning (**Figure 3**).

9   Clip the bottom corners at an angle. Press the seams open. Do not turn right-side out.

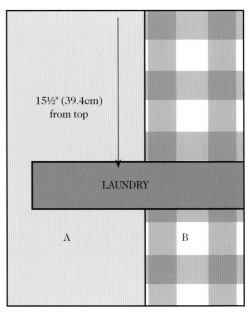

15½" (39.4cm) from top

LAUNDRY

A

B

Figure 2

10 Place the laundry bag inside of the lining, right sides together. Pin the 2 layers along the top edge, aligning the side seams. Sew using a ½" (1.3cm) seam allowance. Press the seam open.

11 Turn the laundry bag with lining right-side out, and whipstitch the opening in the lining. Tuck the lining inside the laundry bag. Press the top edge of the laundry bag.

12 On the casing strip (piece E), press in ¼" (6mm) on each short end. Stitch ⅛" (3mm) from the edge on both ends of the strip (**Figure 4**).

13 Press the casing in half width-wise. Open the strip. Fold each long side in to meet the center crease in the strip and press. Turn the strip over to the right side and press. The casing strip should measure 1½" (3.8cm) wide.

14 Measure 3" (7.6cm) down from the top front edge of the bag. Lay one long edge of the casing strip on this 3" (7.6cm) line, starting at the left bag seam (Figure 5) and continuing around the back. Pin the casing in place, periodically making sure it is 3" (7.6cm) from the top. Stitch down ⅛" (3mm) from the edge on each long side of the casing.

15 To create the tie, sew 2 F strips on the diagonal, right sides together.

16 Trim the seam to leave a ¼" (6mm) seam allowance, and press open.

17 Turn under ¼" (6mm) on each end of the strip. Press the strip in half width-wise. Open the strip up with the wrong side facing up.

18 Fold each long side over 1" (2.5cm) to align with the crease in the center of the strip.

19 Press the strip in half again. All edges should be turned under. Stitch ⅛" (3mm) along the ends and bottom edge of the strip to create the tie.

20 Press the tie for a clean finish. Feed the tie through the casing, and draw the gathers in evenly to complete the laundry bag.

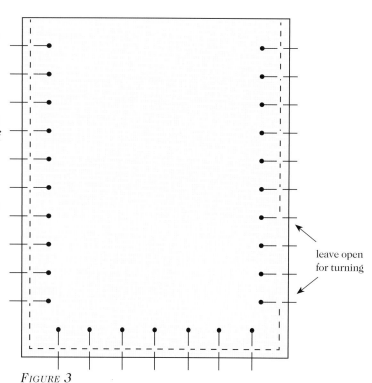

leave open for turning

FIGURE 3

FIGURE 4

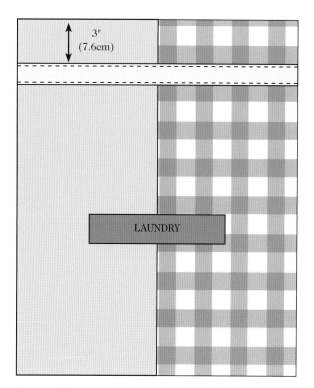

3" (7.6cm)

LAUNDRY

FIGURE 5

Framed Laundry Piece

When I was in my early twenties, I was lucky enough to live in my father's homeland, Montevideo, Uruguay. I spent a great deal of time at my aunt's beach house. She would wash the clothes by hand and let them air-dry in the afternoon sun. This embroidered piece takes me back to that special place.

SUPPLIES

- Fat quarter (18" × 22"/ 45.7cm × 55.9cm) fabric for embroidery background
- Embroidery floss, Anchor colors #62, #73, #77, #128, #169, #254, #400, #1038
- Scrap Form-Flex, at least 13" × 11" (33.0cm × 27.9cm)
- Batting scrap measuring at least 8" × 10" (20.3cm × 25.4cm)
- Quilting thread, neutral color
- Spray paint, light blue
- Picture frame with glass: 8" × 10" (20.3cm × 25.4cm)
- General embroidery supplies, as listed on page 12
- Pattern on page 131

Cutting Instructions

Cut embroidery background to 13" × 11" (33.0cm × 27.9cm)

Cut batting to 10" × 8" (25.4cm × 20.3cm)

1   Place the embroidery template from page 131 on a light box.

2   Lay the background fabric over the image. Trace the image onto the background fabric using the fabric pencil. Iron Form-Flex to wrong side of background fabric.

3   Embroider the image using the stem stitch and 2 strands of floss. The bird beaks require only 1 strand of floss.

Use color 63 for the clothespins; dress collar, cuffs, buttons and pleat lines; underwear (no dots); tank top stripes.

Use color 73 for the dress outline and towel.

Use color 77 for the bird beaks and underwear with dots.

Use color 169 for the blue jeans; bird head and wings; sock toe and heel.

Use color 254 for the grass line; skirt waistband and 2 stripes; tank top outline and stripes.

Use color 400 for the clothesline; bird eyes; wash tub outline.

Use color 1038 for the bird bodies and tail feathers; skirt outline; sock; wash tub band.

Use color 128 for the bubbles.

4   When the embroidery is complete, trim the background fabric to 12" × 10" (30.5cm × 25.4cm).

5   Remove the glass from the frame and set the frame aside.

6   Lay the embroidery piece wrong-side up. Lay the batting on top of the embroidery piece. Lay the glass on top of the batting.

7   Carefully pull the excess embroidery background fabric up over the glass to the back side of the glass.

8   Using a needle and a long piece of quilting thread, stitch from one side of turned fabric across the glass to the other side of turned fabric (**Figure 1**). With each long stitch, carefully pull the fabric taut to make it fit snugly against the glass.

9   Before stitching the remaining 2 sides, fold the corners (**Figure 2**). Then fold the fabric around the glass to create a mitered corner (**Figure 3**). You may use a pin to hold the miter in place while stitching.

10 Complete the remaining 2 sides by stitching vertically across the first set of stitches. Turn the piece over occasionally to ensure the front of the piece is centered and fitting snugly against the glass.

11 Remove the pins.

12 Paint the frame with spray paint in a well-ventilated area. Let it dry for several hours.

13 Carefully insert the embroidery piece into the frame. Attach the back of the frame.

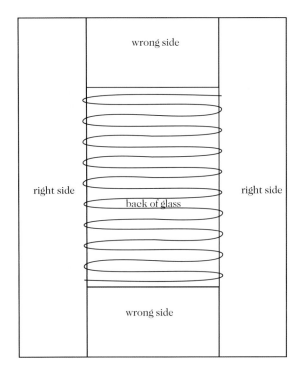

FIGURE 1

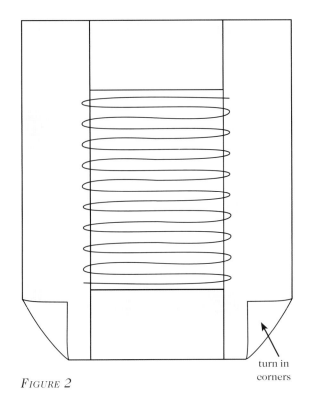

FIGURE 2

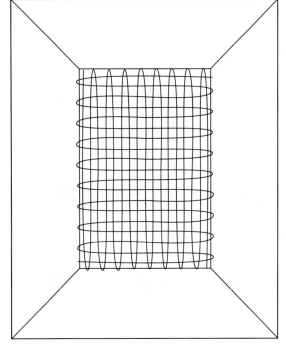

FIGURE 3

Purse Sachet

Nothing is prettier than the sweet scent of lavender as you enter the bathroom. This lovely purse sachet is an extra-special accent, perfect for hanging from a vintage doorknob. It is simple to sew and makes a lovely gift for your mother or a special friend.

SUPPLIES

- Fat eighths (9" × 22"/ 22.9cm × 55.9cm) of 5 coordinating fabrics
- 7" (17.8cm) ribbon, ¼" (6mm) wide
- Decorative button
- Dried lavender
- General patchwork supplies, as listed on page 16

CUTTING INSTRUCTIONS

From Fabric 1:
Cut 1 A: 5½" × 3" (14.0cm × 7.6cm)

From Fabric 2:
Cut 2 B strips: 5½" × 3¾" (14.0cm × 9.5cm)

From Fabric 3:
Cut 2 C strips: 5½" × 1½" (14.0cm × 3.8cm)
Cut 2 D strips for straps: 9½" × 3" (24.1cm × 7.6cm)

From Fabric 4:
Cut 1 E for lining: 5½" × 11½" (14.0cm × 29.2cm)

From Fabric 5:
Cut 2 F pieces for sachet pillow: 5" × 5¾" (12.7cm × 14.6cm)

1. Using a ¼" (6mm) seam allowance, join strips A, B and C together (**Figure 1**). Press the seams in one direction.

2. Stitch the decorative ribbon along the C/B seam at the top of the purse (**Figure 2**).

3. With right sides together, fold the purse in half. Pin. Using a ¼" (6mm) seam allowance, stitch along the sides leaving the top edge open. Turn right-side out, and press the side seams. Set aside.

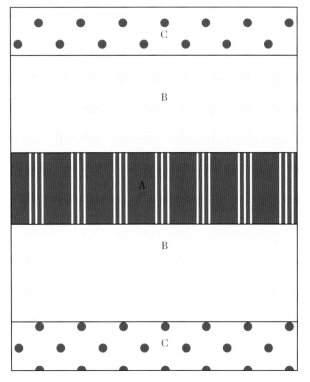

FIGURE 1

add ribbon

FIGURE 2

4   Fold the lining in half, right sides together. Sew along the sides and bottom, using a ¼" (6mm) seam allowance and leaving a small gap open for turning (**Figure 3**).

5   To make the straps, press 1 D strip in half width-wise. Open the strip up with the wrong side facing up.

6   Fold over ¾" (1.9cm) along each long side of the strip. Press. The raw edges of the strip should align with the crease in the center of the strip.

7   Press the strip in half again. The strap should measure ¾" (1.9cm) wide. Stitch ⅛" (3mm) in along the open edge to create the strap. Topstitch ⅛" (3mm) in along the long side of the strap. Repeat steps 5–7 for the remaining strap.

8   Pin one end of the strap on each top edge of the purse, ¾" (1.9cm) in from the side edge (**Figure 4**). Baste the straps in place.

9   Place the purse inside the lining, right sides together. The straps will be inside the lining, too. Pin along the top edge. Stitch the top edge using a ¼" (6mm) seam allowance. Turn the purse right-side out through the opening in the lining. Whipstitch the opening in the lining closed (**Figure 5**).

10 Tuck the lining inside the purse, and press the top edge carefully.

11 Attach the decorative button, centering it on the front side of the purse along the C/B seam.

12 Lay the 2 pieces for the sachet pillow right sides together. Sew using a ¼" (6mm) seam allowance, leaving a 3" (7.6cm) opening on one side for filling. Turn right-side out. Press.

13 Fill the pillow with dried lavender. Whipstitch the opening closed.

14 Gently stuff the pillow inside the purse. Hide the stitched edge inside the purse.

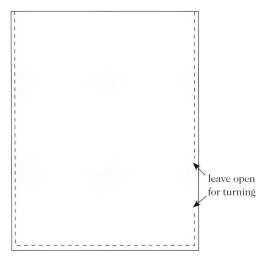

leave open for turning

FIGURE 3

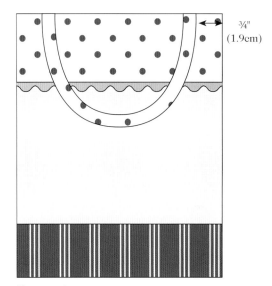

¾" (1.9cm)

FIGURE 4

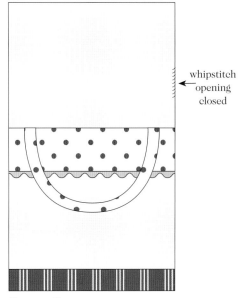

whipstitch opening closed

FIGURE 5

Fabric Shower Curtain

What better way to add charm to your bathroom than with this simple, yet pretty, shower curtain? Feature six of your favorite romantic fabrics in this easy patchwork strip pattern. Mix in a few large-scale prints, and watch the room come alive. This is a wonderful project for any home.

FINISHED SIZE

- 75" × 74½" (1.9m × 1.9m)

SUPPLIES

- 2⅛ yards (1.9m) of 5 different fabrics for shower panel (Fabrics 1–5)

- ⅔ yard (0.6m) fabric for top casing (Fabric 6)

- 4¼ yards (3.9m) fabric for lining (Fabric 7)

- ⅝ yard (0.6m) medium- or heavyweight fusible interfacing, 20" (50.8cm) wide

- General patchwork supplies, as listed on page 16

CUTTING INSTRUCTIONS

From Fabrics 1 and 5:

Cut 1 piece: 9¼" × 75" (23.5cm × 190.5cm)
Cut 1 piece: 8" × 75" (20.3cm × 190.5cm)

From Fabrics 2, 3 and 4:

Cut 2 pieces: 8" × 75" (20.3cm × 190.5cm)

From Fabric 6:

Cut 2 strips for top casing: WOF × 11" (WOF × 27.9cm)

From Fabric 7:

Cut 2 lining pieces: 38½" × 74" (97.8cm × 188.0cm)

From Interfacing:

Cut 4 strips for top casing: 18¾" × 5" (47.6cm × 12.7cm)

Note: Use a ¼" (6mm) seam allowance, unless otherwise noted. Backstitch at the beginning and end of each seam.

1. Turn under ¾" (1.9cm) of one long side of the 9¼" × 75" (23.5cm × 190.5cm) piece of Fabric 1. Press. Turn under ¾" (1.9cm) again and press. Edgestitch. Repeat for the same size piece of Fabric 5.

2. Stitch the hemmed Fabric 1 piece to the left side of one Fabric 2 panel (**Figure 1**). Press the seam open.

3. Stitch one Fabric 3 panel to the right side of the Fabric 1/2 unit. Press the seam open.

4. Stitch one Fabric 4 panel to the right side of the Fabric 1/2/3 unit. Press the seam open.

5. Stitch the unfinished Fabric 5 panel to the right side of the Fabric 1/2/3/4 unit. Press the seam open. This is Unit A; set it aside.

6. Stitch the hemmed Fabric 5 piece to the right side of the second Fabric 4 panel. Press the seam open.

7. Stitch the second Fabric 3 panel to the left side of the Fabric 4/5 unit. Press the seam open.

8. Stitch the second Fabric 2 panel to the left side of the Fabric 3/4/5 unit. Press the seam open.

9. Stitch the remaining Fabric 1 panel to the left side of the Fabric 2/3/4/5 unit. Press the seam open. This is Unit B.

10. Stitch Unit A to Unit B. Press the seam open. If necessary, trim the top and bottom edges to be even.

11. Turn under ¾" (1.9cm) along the bottom edge of the shower curtain panel; press. Turn up 4" (10.2cm); press. Edgestitch along the side, pivot at the 4" (10.2cm) hem, edgestitch along the whole hem, pivot at the side, and edgestitch to the bottom of the curtain.

12. For the lining, turn under ¾" (1.9cm) on one long side of each panel; press. Turn under ¾" (1.9cm) again, and press. Edgestitch.

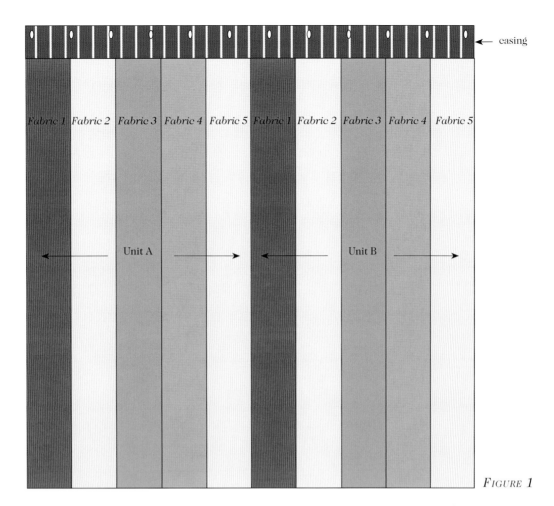

← casing

Fabric 1 | *Fabric 2* | *Fabric 3* | *Fabric 4* | *Fabric 5* | *Fabric 1* | *Fabric 2* | *Fabric 3* | *Fabric 4* | *Fabric 5*

← Unit A → ← Unit B →

FIGURE 1

13　Stitch the lining panels together along the unfinished edges. Press the seam open.

14　Turn under ¾" (1.9cm) along the bottom edge of the lining; press. Turn up 4" (10.2cm); press. Edgestitch.

15　With the wrong sides together, line up the top of the shower curtain and the top of the lining. The lining should fit inside the 2 hemmed edges of the shower curtain.

16　Baste the shower curtain and the lining together along the top edge using a ⅛" (3mm) seam.

17　Trim the selvages from both top casing strips. Cut each strip to measure 39¼" (99.7cm). Stitch the strips together along one short side; press the seam open.

18　Turn under ¾" (1.9cm) on one long side and both short sides of the casing strip; press. Do not stitch.

19　Line up the interfacing strips end-to-end inside the folded edges of the casing strip. Attach the interfacing following the manufacturer's

instructions. Re-press the folded edges of the casing strip.

20　Fold the side without the interfacing over onto the top of the interfaced side; press.

21　Lay the right side of the non-interfaced side of the casing onto the right side of the patchwork side of the shower curtain. Stitch the casing onto the shower curtain; press the seam toward the casing.

22　Starting at the lower edge of the casing, edgestitch around all 4 sides of the casing.

23　To add buttonholes to hang the curtain, mark 2¼" (5.7cm) in from each end of the casing. Measure and mark 6" (15.2cm) from one of these marks, and continue to make marks every 6" (15.2cm) until you reach the mark on the other end of the casing. There will be a total of 12 marks. At each mark, make a buttonhole, following the instructions for your sewing machine, ⅞" (2.2cm) long with the top of the hole starting 1¼" (3.2cm) from the top of the casing.

Mini Appliqué Vignette

I love things that contain other things. I am always on the hunt for unique items for my home, which includes décor that's a mix of old and new. I fell in love with this memory box because it was the perfect way to feature a charming appliqué. The simple dress form with accent roses sits beautifully in this setting.

FINISHED SIZE

- 8" × 10" (20.3cm × 25.4cm)

SUPPLIES

- 12" × 8¾" (30.5cm × 22.2cm) fabric scrap for background
- 12" × 2" (30.5cm × 5.1cm) fabric scrap for background
- 12" × 5½" (30.5cm × 14.0cm) fabric scrap for background
- Scraps for various appliqué shapes
- Embroidery floss, Anchor colors #57, #926, #943
- 8" × 10" (20.3cm × 25.4cm) shadowbox frame
- General appliqué supplies, as listed on page 8
- General embroidery supplies, as listed on page 12
- Pattern on page 133

1   Join the 3 backgrounds along the 12" (30.5cm) side.
    Press the seams down.

2   Appliqué the shapes using the pattern on page 133 and
    following the appliqué steps on pages 9–11 as a guide.

3   Mark the embroidery lines using the fabric pencil.

4   Embroider using 2 strands of embroidery floss,
    following the embroidery steps on pages 13–15 as a
    guide. For the hanger and leaf stem, use the stem stitch
    and floss 943. For the ribbon, use the stem stitch and
    floss 57. For the border, use the stem stitch and floss
    926; use this floss for the French knots as well.

5   Once the appliqué and embroidery are complete, press
    the block from the back to smooth any unevenness.

6   Carefully remove the padded area from the shadowbox
    frame. This may require some effort because it may
    have an adhesive holding it in place.

7   Lay the block wrong-side up. Lay the right side of the
    padded area onto the block. Make sure to center the
    block.

8   Pull the fabric around to the wrong side of the padded
    area. Use appliqué pins to hold the fabric in place.
    Start pinning in the corners first, then carefully work
    your way around the edges until all the edges have
    been held down.

9   Set the pad back into the frame.

10 Carefully remove the glass from the frame and discard.

Relaxing and Resting

Whether taking a few hours to yourself or enjoying several days of R & R, the items you learn to make in this chapter can make that time more enjoyable. In the coming pages, you will learn to make a beautiful *Artist Journal Cover*, a dainty *Pedestal Pincushion* and a delightful *Patchwork Memory Board*. All will make your creative time something to enjoy. Or maybe you prefer to spend your free hours outside picking blooms with your pretty *Garden Tote* or lunching in the backyard on your *Patchwork Picnic Quilt*.

Then you might retire in the evening to curl up under the delicate *Appliqué Bed Quilt* to read your favorite novel. However you choose to spend your time, these projects are all perfect for relaxing and resting.

Artist Journal Cover

When I was seven, my very first art teacher introduced me to the artist journal. She taught me to sketch and keep my ideas inside and to always keep one going. I have done just that and am rarely without one. I decided to create a journal cover so the outside could be a form of expression, too. The embroidered word *dream* encourages the maker to do just that.

SUPPLIES

- ⅜ yard (0.4m) fabric for back of journal
- Fat eighth (9" × 22"/ 22.9cm × 55.9cm) appliqué background fabric
- Fat eighth (9" × 22"/ 22.9cm × 55.9cm) journal accent fabric
- Assorted fabric scraps for patchwork and appliqué
- Embroidery floss, Anchor colors #77, #358
- 1 yard (0.9m) ribbon for ties, 1" (2.5cm) wide
- ½ yard (0.5m) ribbon for accent, 1" (2.5cm) wide
- 2 black beads, 2mm
- 8½" × 11" (21.6cm × 27.9cm) artist's sketchbook
- Batting scrap, cotton or low loft, measuring at least 12" × 27" (30.5cm × 68.6cm)
- Optional: Vintage rose appliqué
- General appliqué supplies, as listed on page 8
- General embroidery supplies, as listed on page 12
- General patchwork supplies, as listed on page 16
- Patterns on pages 122–123

Cutting Instructions

From the appliqué background fabric, cut A: 8¼" × 10¼" (21.0cm × 26.0cm)

From the scrap fabrics, choose 9 fabrics and assign a letter B–J to each. Then make the following cuts.
Cut B: 7¼" × 1¼" (18.4cm × 3.2cm)
Cut C: 2⅛" × 2⅜" (5.4cm × 6.0cm)
Cut D: 2⅛" × 2⅜" (5.4cm × 6.0cm)
Cut E: 2⅛" × 2⅜" (5.4cm × 6.0cm)
Cut F: 2⅛" × 2⅜" (5.4cm × 6.0cm)
Cut G: 2⅞" × 12¼" (7.3cm × 31.1cm)
Cut H for back panel: 9¾" × 12¼" (24.8cm × 31.1cm)
Cut I for side panel: 4½" × 12¼" (11.4cm × 31.1cm).
Cut J for lining: 26¾" × 12¼" (68.0cm × 31.1cm)

From the batting scrap, cut 1 piece: 26" × 11⅜" (66.0cm × 28.9cm)

1 Appliqué the image on Fabric A (appliqué background) following the appliqué instructions on pages 9–11 and the pattern on page 123.

2 Embroider the word *Dream* following the embroidery instructions on page 13 and the pattern on page 122. Use the stem stitch to embroider both the word and the bird's feet. Use the chain stitch to embroider the birdhouse chain. Attach the beads for the bird's eyes.

To make a chain stitch, bring your needle up through your starting point. Put the needle down just slightly to the right of where you brought it up, then bring it up through the next point. Make sure your thread is under the needle, then pull the thread through. You have made one chain stitch. Put your needle down through the same hole that you just pulled through. Bring your needle up for the next stitch, make sure the thread is under your needle and pull through. To end the chain, just put your needle down through on the other side of the chain you just made; pull through and make a small knot on the wrong side.

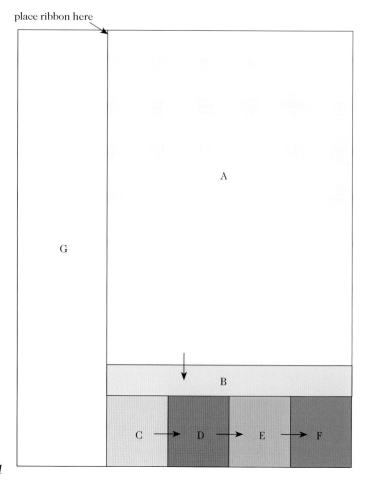

FIGURE 1

3   Trim the appliqué background (A) to 7¼" × 9¼" (18.4cm × 23.5cm).

4   Stitch the following units together using a ¼" (6mm) seam allowance to create the top part of the journal cover (**Figure 1**).
Join the top of B to the bottom of A. Press the seam toward B.
Join the right side of C to the left side of D. Press the seam toward D.
Join the right side of D to the left side of E. Press the seam toward E.
Join the right side of E to the left side of F. Press the seam toward F.
Join the top of C/D/E/F unit to the bottom of A/B unit. Press the seam toward B.
Join the right side of G to the left side of appliqué unit. Press the seam toward G.
Join the right side of piece H (back panel) to the left side of G. Press the seam toward H.
Join the left side of I (side panel) to the right side of appliqué unit. Press the seam toward I.

5   Measure from the top edge of the cover to the bottom edge. Cut the accent ribbon to this length. Place the accent ribbon over the seam between G and the appliqué unit. Stitch down each long side of the ribbon to secure it in place.

6   Press under a ¼" (6mm) seam allowance on each side edge of the cover, and stitch a small hem.

7   Press under a ¼" (6mm) seam allowance on each side edge of the cover lining, and stitch a small hem.

8   Lay the journal cover and lining right sides together and pin. Stitch the top and bottom of cover using a ¼" (6mm) seam allowance. Leave the ends open so the journal cover is a tube.

9   Turn right-side out and press.

10 Carefully insert the batting into the cover.

11 Slide the cover over the journal, inserting one end carefully and then the other. Adjust until the cover fits nicely. Press from the front using care. This will create creases at the cover edges that indicate where the fabric folds over to make the flaps.

12 Remove the journal. Find the midpoint of each flap and center the ribbon wrong-side up (**Figure 2**). Stitch from the edge of the flap to the crease. Use care to stitch through the journal cover and batting only; do not stitch through the lining.

13 Carefully slide the journal into the cover and ease to fit. Tie the ribbon ties into a bow.

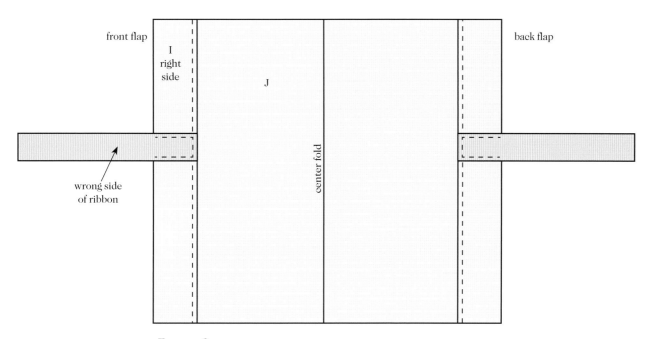

FIGURE 2

Pedestal Pincushion

This darling pincushion is made from simple elements and can display your favorite sewing items. With a beautiful embroidered rose, this will be the prettiest accent in any sewing room. A simple construction makes this a wonderful project to make for yourself or a friend.

SUPPLIES

- 9" × 9" (22.9cm × 22.9cm) fabric for embroidery background
- 9" × 9" (22.9cm × 22.9cm) Form-Flex
- 1 yard (0.9m) decorative ribbon, 1½" (3.8cm) wide
- ½ yard (0.5m) tiny rickrack
- Embroidery floss, Anchor colors #48, #57, #77, #78, #257, #265, #271
- 2 decorative straight pins
- Vintage spools or other items to display
- Mason jar, standard size, with lid
- 4" (10.2cm) glass candlestick
- Sawdust
- Plastic wrap
- Glass glue
- Small rubber band
- General embroidery supplies, as listed on page 12
- Patterns on pages 130, 137

1   Using the marking pencil, trace the rose embroidery image from page 130 onto the right side of the background fabric square.

2   Iron the Form-Flex to the wrong side of the fabric square.

3   Following the marked guidelines, embroider the rose image using 1 strand of embroidery floss and the satin stitch, unless otherwise noted.
Use color 78 for the center of the rose.
Use colors 48, 57, 77 and 271 for the assorted rose petals.
Use color 257 for the stem and leaves.
Use color 265 for the leaf accents.

4   Once the embroidery is complete, press the fabric from the wrong side. Set aside.

5   Trace the circle template from page 137 onto the matte side of the freezer paper. Cut out on the template lines.

6   Lay the template shiny-side down over the wrong side of the embroidery, centering the rose. Press. Cut the fabric out around the edge of the template.

7   Cut 2 small pieces of plastic wrap, each approximately 10" × 10" (25.4cm × 25.4cm). Lay one on top of the other. Pour ½ to 1 cup sawdust onto the plastic wrap, then pull the sides up to enclose the sawdust. Use the small rubber band to secure the plastic wrap closed. Be careful not to use too much sawdust.

8   Turn the sawdust package over and form it into a slightly flattened ball.

9   Twist off the lid to the Mason jar.

10 Using the glass glue, glue the top of the glass candlestick to the bottom of the Mason jar. Let dry.

11 Once the glue is dry, fill the jar with items you want to display.

12 Set the sawdust ball, rubber band-side down, onto the metal side of the circle that pops out of the Mason jar lid.

13 Lay the embroidered circle over the sawdust ball. Pull the fabric edges over the ball.

14 Carefully push the embroidered ball through the opening in the Mason jar lid. Pull the fabric edges down around the metal circle.

15 Set the lid onto the Mason jar and carefully twist it closed. The fabric should extend over the sides of the jar. If the lid does not fit properly, your sawdust ball is too large.

16 Using sharp-tipped scissors, carefully trim away the excess fabric.

17 Place the tiny rickrack at the very edge of the fabric on the lid, butting it up against the metal rim. Attach with small drops of glue on the fabric, working a small area at a time.

18 Tie the ribbon into a bow around the stem of the candlestick. Insert 2 decorative pins into the pincushion.

TIP: Glass candlesticks can be purchased at most craft stores, or pick up a vintage one from an antique store or flea market. Or you can opt to not use a candlestick at all, and simply use only the Mason jar.

Fabric Coasters

One of my favorite things to do is casually entertain in my garden. These fabric coasters are the perfect way to add a little romance to my vintage-inspired patio table. Using a simple reverse appliqué technique and a bit of embroidery, these darling coasters set off a beautiful rose fabric, not to mention provide a pretty place to set your favorite glassware.

SUPPLIES FOR 4 COASTERS

- ¼ yard (0.2m) fabric for strip and backing (Fabric 1)
- ¼ yard (0.2m) fabric for background (Fabric 2)
- ¼ yard (0.2m) fabric for rose shapes or 4 roses, each measuring 6" × 8" (15.2cm × 20.3cm) (Fabric 3)
- 2½ yards (2.3m) rickrack
- Embroidery floss, Anchor color #62
- Embroidery needle
- General appliqué supplies, as listed on page 8
- General embroidery supplies, as listed on page 12
- General patchwork supplies, as listed on page 16
- Pattern on page 128

Cutting Instructions

From Fabric 1:
Cut 8 A strips: 6" × 3¾" (15.2cm × 9.5cm)

From Fabric 2:
Cut 4 B strips: 6" × 1½" (15.2cm × 3.8cm)
Cut 8 D squares for backing: 5½"× 5½" (14.0cm × 14.0cm)

From Fabric 3:
Cut 4 C pieces, making sure to center the floral motif: 6" × 8" (15.2cm × 20.3cm)

1   Sew 1 A strip to each side of 1 B strip. Press the seam toward the B strip.

2   Trace the opening template onto the matte side of the freezer paper. Cut out on the line using paper scissors.

3   Fold the A/B unit in half and press. Fold the A/B unit in half again in the opposite direction and press. This will help center the freezer paper template. Unfold the A/B unit.

4   Using the creases as guidelines, iron the freezer paper template onto the right side of the A/B unit. Trace around the template using a fabric pencil (**Figure 1**). Remove the template.

5   Lay piece C right-side up. Lay the A/B unit with the marking on top, right-side up. Baste the 2 pieces together around the outside edge.

6   From the A/B unit only, cut a scant ¼" (6mm) inside the marking, cutting out the template shape. Use caution not to clip piece C.

7   Using the marked line as the guide, needleturn under the A/B unit edge, revealing the floral motif underneath. Continue to appliqué around the entire template shape.

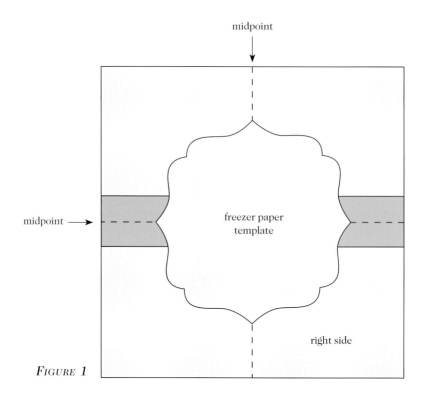

Figure 1

8   Using 2 strands of embroidery floss, stem stitch along the inside edge of the appliquéd shape.

9   Baste the rickrack along the right side of the coaster using a ¼" (6mm) seam allowance. The rickrack should align with the edge of the coaster (**Figure 2**).

10 Turn under a ½" (1.3cm) hem on 1 side of each D piece and press. Stitch the hem with a ⅜" (1cm) seam allowance.

11 With right sides up, lay 1 D piece over another D piece, overlapping the 2 pieces 1½" (3.8cm). Baste from the top edge to the bottom edge of the pieces (**Figure 3**).

12 Lay the front of the coaster and basted backs right sides together, centering the overlapped opening. Pin and stitch the 2 together using a ¼" (6mm) seam allowance.

13 Remove the basting stitches, clip the corners and turn right-side out through the opening in the back. Press from both sides.

14 Topstitch from the top side of the coaster ⅛" (3mm) from the edge for a nice clean finish. Repeat steps 1–14 for the additional 3 coasters.

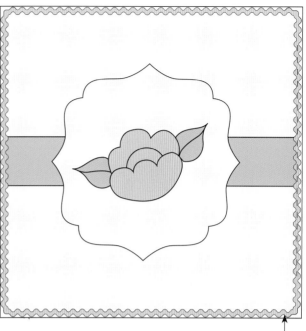

FIGURE 2   baste rickrack

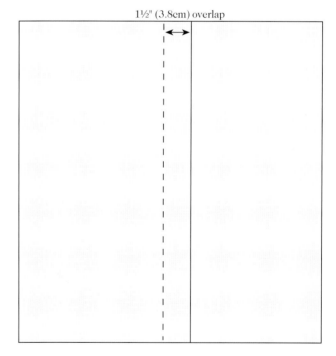

FIGURE 3

Garden Tote

One of my favorite things to do is to go to my garden and cut fresh flowers to enjoy in my home. This lovely floral garden tote not only holds your favorite garden tools, but it is the perfect holder for fresh-cut blooms. It's easy to make, too, and fun to give to your favorite gardening friend.

SUPPLIES

- ¼ yard (0.2m) fabric for gusset (Fabric 1)
- ⅝ yard (0.6m) fabric for side panels and pockets (Fabric 2)
- ¼ yard (0.2m) fabric for pockets (Fabric 3)
- ½ yard (0.5m) fabric for binding and ruffle (Fabric 4)
- ¼ yard (0.2m) fabric for straps (Fabric 5)
- 1⅛ yards (1.0m) fabric for lining (Fabric 6)
- 4 yards (3.7m) Form-Flex
- 4 fabric-covered buttons, ¾" (1.9cm)
- Illustration board or heavyweight interfacing (such as Timtex or Fast2Fuse), 15" × 20" (38.1cm × 50.8cm)
- General patchwork supplies, as listed on page 16

CUTTING INSTRUCTIONS

From Fabric 1:
Cut 1 A strip: 4½" × 42" (11.4cm × 106.7cm)

From Fabric 2:
Cut 2 B pieces: 16" × 14" (40.6cm × 35.6cm)
Cut 4 C pieces: 6" × 9" (15.2cm × 22.9cm)

From Fabric 3:
Cut 2 D pieces: 6" × 9" (15.2cm × 22.9cm)

From Fabric 4:
Cut 2 E strips: 6" × 44" (15.2cm × 111.8cm)
Cut 2 F strips: 3¼" × 16" (8.3cm × 40.6cm)

From Fabric 5:
Cut 2 G strips for straps: 2½" × 34" (6.4cm × 86.4cm)

From Fabric 6:
Cut 2 pocket lining pieces: 16" × 9" (40.6cm × 22.9cm)
Cut 1 strip lining: 4½" × 42" (11.4cm × 106.7cm)
Cut 2 lining pieces: 16" × 14" (40.6cm × 35.6cm)
Cut 2 strap lining pieces: 2½" × 34" (6.4cm × 86.4cm)
Cut 2 pieces to cover base insert: 4⅜" × 15⅝" (11.1cm × 39.7cm)

From Illustration Board:
Cut 1 strip for inside bottom of bag: 3⅜" × 14⅝" (8.6cm × 37.1cm)

Note: Use a ½" (1.3cm) seam allowance unless otherwise noted.

1   Back pieces A, B, C and D, as well as all lining pieces, with Form-Flex.

2   To create the pocket panel, sew 1 C piece to each side of 1 D piece along the 9" (22.9cm) sides. Press the seams open. Repeat with the remaining C and D pieces for the second pocket panel.

3   With wrong sides together, sew the pocket panel front to the pocket panel lining on all 4 sides, using a ¼" (6mm) seam allowance. Repeat for the second pocket panel.

4   Fold the F strip width-wise, wrong sides together. Do not press.

5   To create the pocket panel binding, lay the folded strip onto the lining side of 1 pocket panel, right sides together and raw edges aligned. Sew along this edge with a ½" (1.3cm) seam allowance (**Figure 1**).

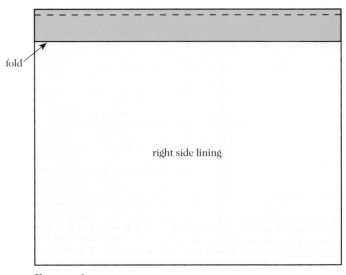

fold

right side lining

FIGURE 1

6 Press the folded strip over to the right side of the pocket panel. Stitch down onto the front of the pocket panel, ⅛" (3mm) from the edge of the binding (**Figure 2**). Repeat steps 4–6 with the second side panel and the second F strip.

7 Lay the wrong side of the pocket panel onto the right side of the side panel B. Pin. Baste along the 3 sides of the pocket panel using a ¼" (6mm) seam allowance.

8 To create the pockets, stitch from the top edge of the pocket panel binding to the bottom edge of the side panel through all thicknesses, following seam lines of C/D units (**Figure 3**).

9 Now the gusset piece D needs to be set in. I highly recommend basting all gusset seams prior to doing the final stitching.

10 Join 1 side of the gusset to the side panel of the bag, right sides together. Start at the top of the bag and stop ½" (1.3cm) from the bottom of the bag (**Figure 4**). Press the seam open.

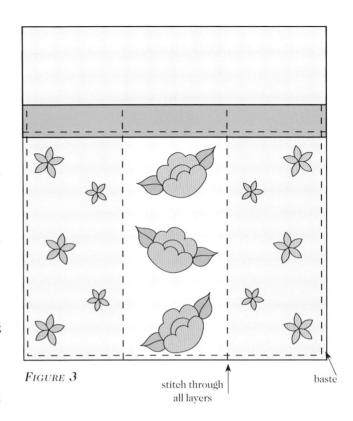

FIGURE 3

stitch through all layers

baste

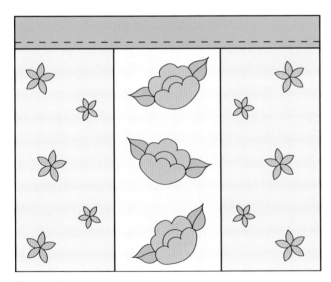

FIGURE 2

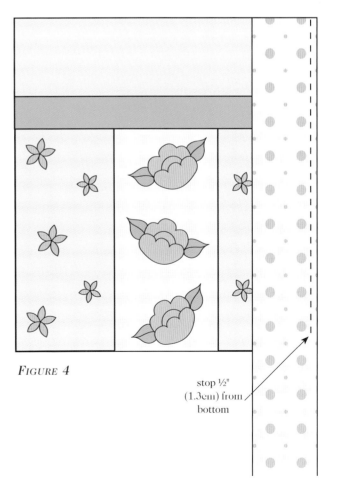

FIGURE 4

stop ½" (1.3cm) from bottom

11 Sew the gusset to bottom of the bag, once again with right sides together and starting ½" (1.3cm) in from the bottom right edge and stopping ½" (1.3cm) from the bottom left edge (**Figure 5**). Press the seam open.

12 Sew the remaining side of the gusset, right sides together starting ½" (1.3cm) from the bottom of the bag. Continue sewing up to the top edge of the bag (**Figure 6**). Press the seam open.

13 Repeat steps 10–12 to sew the gusset to the second side panel.

14 To make the ruffle, join 1 E strip to another E strip, right sides together sewing on the diagonal. Press the seam open. Trim the seam to ¼" (6mm).

15 Square up both ends of the long strip to clean up the edges. Turn under ¼" (6mm) on each end of the strip and sew a small hem.

16 Fold the long strip in half width-wise. Press.

17 Along the raw edge, sewing both edges together, sew a basting line of stitches ¼" (6mm) from the raw edge. Sew another basting line of stitches ⅜" (1cm) from the edges. Gather the stitches until the ruffle measures 38" (96.5cm).

18 Starting pinning the ruffle 4" (10.2cm) from the edge of the bag. Align the raw edge of the ruffle with the raw edge at the top of the back, and pin with right sides together all the way around the outside top edge of the bag. Overlap the ends of the ruffle slightly. When the ruffle is pinned and evenly spaced, baste in place using a ⅜" (1cm) seam allowance.

19 To create the lining, follow steps 9–13. The only difference is that on one side of the lining, leave a small 4" (10.2cm) gap unsewn. This will allow for turning the bag later.

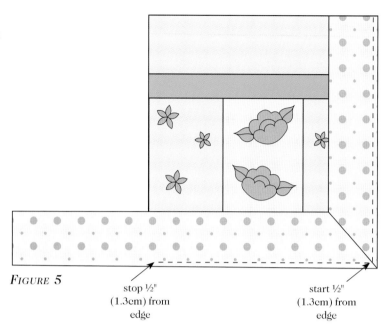

FIGURE 5

stop ½" (1.3cm) from edge

start ½" (1.3cm) from edge

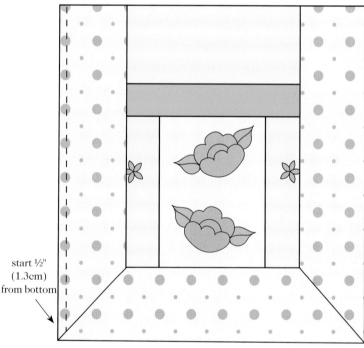

start ½" (1.3cm) from bottom

FIGURE 6

20 Place the bag right-side out inside the lining, which is wrong-side out. The bag and lining will have right sides together. Align the top edges and match up the seams. Pin in place. Stitch the top edge seam using a ½" (1.3cm) seam allowance.

21 Trim the seam allowance to ¼" (6mm) to reduce bulk. Turn the bag right-side out. Whipstitch the opening in the lining closed.

22 To create the straps, put strap piece G and the strap lining right sides together. Pin and stitch the strap using a ½" (1.3cm) seam allowance along 3 sides, leaving 1 short end open for turning.

23 Trim the seam allowance to ¼" (6mm). Turn the strap right-side out and press.

24 Turn under ½" (1.3cm) at the open end of the strap and press. Topstitch the strap ⅛" (3mm) from the edge on all 4 sides. Repeat steps 22–24 for the remaining strap.

25 Pin the lining side of one end of a strap to the right side of the bag. Place the end of the strap 3" (7.6cm) down from the top edge of the bag. Align the inside edge of the strap with the pocket seam. Pin in place. Place the other end of the strap on the same side of the bag, 3" (7.6cm) down from the top edge, aligning the inside edge with the seam on the other side of the pocket (**Figure 7**).

26 Stitch the strap onto the bag following the top stitching on the strap as a guide. Repeat steps 25–26 for the remaining strap.

27 To create the bottom bag insert, sew the 2 bag insert pieces right sides together along 3 sides using a ⅜" (1cm) seam allowance. Leave one short end of the bag unsewn. Trim the seam to ¼" (6mm) and turn right-side out.

28 Carefully slide the illustration board insert into the sleeve. Turn the edges of the open end under and whipstitch the opening closed.

29 Cover 4 buttons with fabric. Stitch 1 button to each end of the straps, placing the button ⅜" (1cm) from the bottom of the strap.

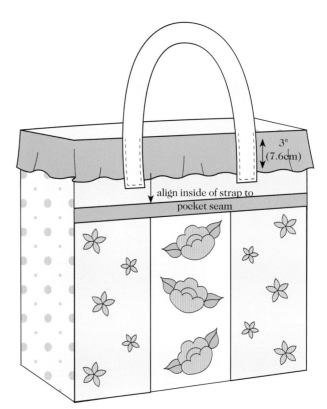

3" (7.6cm)

align inside of strap to pocket seam

FIGURE 7

99

Patchwork Picnic Quilt

What better way to enjoy the garden than having an outdoor picnic on this charming patchwork quilt? This is the perfect beginner's project. It features three great blocks to learn: the Rail Fence, the Nine Patch and the Four Patch. All are set on point in a simple diagonal setting. So easy, yet so charming.

FINISHED SIZE

- 73" × 89" (185.4cm × 226.1cm)

SUPPLIES

- ½ yard (0.5m) fabric for Rail Fence block (Fabric 1)
- ½ yard (0.5m) fabric for Rail Fence block (Fabric 2)
- ½ yard (0.5m) fabric for Rail Fence block (Fabric 3)
- ⅞ yard (0.8m) fabric for Nine Patch block (Fabric 4)
- ¼ yard (0.2m) for Four Patch block (Fabric 5)
- ¼ yard (0.2m) for Four Patch block (Fabric 6)
- 1½ yards (1.4m) fabric for sashing (Fabric 7)
- 1¾ yards (1.6m) for alternate blocks and setting and corner triangles (Fabric 8)
- ⅝ yard (0.6m) fabric for inner border (Fabric 9)
- 1¼ yards (1.1m) fabric for outer border (Fabric 10)
- ⅔ yard (0.6m) fabric for binding
- 5¼ yards (4.8m) fabric for backing
- General patchwork supplies, as listed on page 16

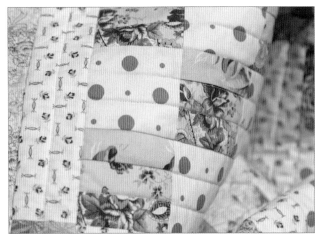

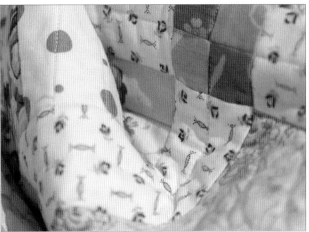

Cutting Instructions

From Fabric 1:
Cut 9 A strips: 1½" × WOF (3.8cm × WOF)

From Fabric 2:
Cut 9 B strips: 1½" × WOF (3.8cm × WOF)

From Fabric 3:
Cut 9 C strips: 1½" × WOF (3.8cm × WOF)

From Fabric 4:
Cut 80 D squares: 3½" × 3½" (8.9cm × 8.9cm)

From Fabric 5:
Cut 3 E strips: 1½" × WOF (3.8cm × WOF)

From Fabric 6:
Cut 3 F strips: 1½" × WOF (3.8cm × WOF)

From Fabric 7:
Cut 80 G strips: 2½" × 9½" (6.4cm × 24.1cm)

From Fabric 8:
Cut 5 H squares: 4¼" × 4¼" (10.8cm × 10.8cm), then cut in half on both diagonals
Cut 12 I squares: 9½" × 9½" (24.1cm × 24.1cm)
Cut 4 J squares: 14¼" × 14¼" (36.2cm × 36.2cm), then cut in half on both diagonals
Cut 2 K squares: 7½" × 7½" (19.1cm × 19.1cm), then cut in half on one diagonal

From Fabric 9:
Cut 4 L strips: 2½" × WOF (6.4cm × WOF)
Cut 4 M strips: 2½" × WOF (6.4cm × WOF)

From Fabric 10:
Cut 4 N strips: 4½" × WOF (11.4cm × WOF)
Cut 4 O strips: 4½" × WOF (11.4cm × WOF)

From Binding Fabric:
Cut strips on the bias: 2⅜" (6.0cm) for a total of 400" (10.2m)

Making 100 Rail Fence Blocks

1. Join 1 strip A, B and C together along the 45" (114.3cm) side. Press toward the B strip.

2. Repeat step 1 for a total of 9 A/B/C strip sets.

3. Cut the strip sets every 3½" (8.9cm) for a total of 100 Rail Fence blocks measuring 3½" × 3½" (8.9cm × 8.9cm) (**Figure 1**).

Making 20 Nine Patch Blocks

1. Join 1 Rail Fence block to each side of 1 D square. Press the seams toward the D square. This creates Nine Patch Unit 1. Repeat this step for a total of 40 units.

2. Join 1 D square to each side of a Rail Fence block. Press the seams toward the D squares. This creates Nine Patch Unit 2. Repeat this step for a total of 20 units.

3. Join 1 Unit 1 to the top and bottom of each Unit 2. Press toward Unit 1. Repeat this step for a total of 20 Nine Patch blocks (**Figure 2**).

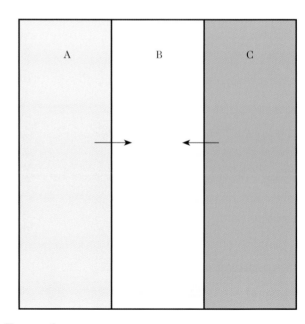

Figure 1

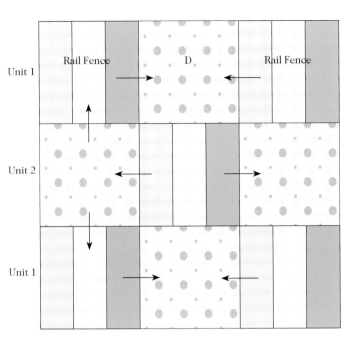

FIGURE 2

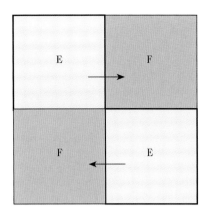

FIGURE 3

MAKING 31 FOUR PATCH BLOCKS

1. Join 1 strip E to 1 strip F along the 45" (114.3cm) side. Press the seam toward F.

2. Repeat step 1 for a total of 3 strip sets.

3. Cut the strip sets every 1½" (3.8cm) for a total of 62 units.

4. Join 2 units together to create a Four Patch block. Repeat this step for a total of 31 Four Patch blocks (**Figure 3**).

JOINING THE BLOCKS INTO ROWS

1. Create 9 Sashing/Four Patch rows. See **Figure 4** to determine how many sashing strips and Four Patch blocks go in each row. Press the seams toward the sashing.

2. Join 1 H triangle to each end of the above 9 rows. Press the seams toward the sashing.

3. Create 8 Sashing/Nine Patch rows. See Figure 4 to determine how many sashing strips and Nine Patches go in each row. Press the seams toward the sashing.

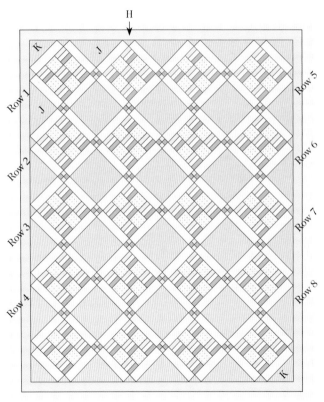

FIGURE 4

4. Join 1 J triangle to each end of the above 8 rows. Press the seams toward the sashing.

5. Join the rows and press the seams toward the sashing.

6. Sew 1 K triangle to each corner to complete the top.

ADDING BORDERS AND FINISHING

1   Join 2 L strips on the diagonal along the 2½" (6.4cm) side. Press seam in one direction, and trim seam allowance to ¼" (6mm). Repeat for the remaining L strips for a total of 2 long L strips.

2   Measure the body of the quilt through the center from top to bottom. Cut each L strip to this measurement.

3   Join 1 L border to each side of the quilt. Press seams toward the L border.

4   Join 2 M strips on the diagonal along the 2½" (6.4cm) side. Press seam in one direction, and trim seam allowance to ¼" (6mm). Repeat for the remaining M strips for a total of 2 long M strips.

5   Measure the body of the quilt through the center from side to side. Cut each M strip to this measurement.

6   Join 1 M border to the top and bottom of the quilt. Press the seams toward M.

7   Join 2 N strips on the diagonal along the 4½" (11.4cm) side. Press seam in one direction, and trim seam allowance to ¼" (6mm). Repeat for the remaining N strips for a total of 2 long N strips.

8   Measure the body of the quilt through the center from top to bottom. Cut each N strip to this measurement.

9   Join 1 N border to each side of the quilt. Press the seams toward N.

10   Join 2 O strips on the diagonal along the 4½" (11.4cm) side. Press seam in one direction, and trim seam allowance to ¼" (6mm). Repeat for the remaining O strips for a total of 2 long O strips.

11   Measure the body of the quilt through the center from side to side. Cut each O strip to this measurement.

12   Join 1 O border to the top and bottom of the quilt. Press the seams toward O.

13   Layer, baste and quilt as desired. Bind using the binding strips joined together on the diagonal.

Patchwork Memory Board

I absolutely love ephemera. This wonderful patchwork memory board is an easy, yet fun way to display personal memories and treasured bits you'd like to save. Romantic fabrics and simple patchwork make for a wonderful beginner's project. Once finished, tack on millinery flowers, postcards, buttons and so much more. Watch this piece come alive with charm.

FINISHED SIZE

- 18" × 24" (45.7m × 61cm)

SUPPLIES

- ¼ yard (0.2m) of 8 different fabrics (Fabrics A–H)
- 18" × 24" (45.7cm × 61.0cm) piece of foam core
- 20" × 26" (50.8cm × 66.0cm) piece of batting
- 4 yards (3.7m) ribbon, medium value, ½" (1.3cm) wide (Ribbon A)
- 4 yards (3.7m) ribbon, dark value, ¼" (6mm) wide (Ribbon B)
- ¾" (1.9cm) appliqué pins
- Masking tape
- Spray adhesive
- Optional: frame 18" × 24" (45.7cm × 61cm)
- Optional: felt or felted wool measuring 20" × 26" (50.8cm × 66.0cm)
- General patchwork supplies, as listed on page 16

CUTTING INSTRUCTIONS

From Fabric A:
Cut 1 rectangle: 5½" × 4½" (14.0cm × 11.4cm)
Cut 3 rectangles: 3½" × 4½" (8.9cm × 11.4cm)
Cut 2 rectangles: 2½" × 3½" (6.4cm × 8.9cm)

From Fabric B:
Cut 1 square: 4½" × 4½" (11.4cm × 11.4cm)
Cut 3 rectangles: 2½" × 4½" (6.4cm × 11.4cm)
Cut 1 rectangle: 3½" × 5½" (8.9cm × 14.0cm)
Cut 1 rectangle: 3½" × 3½" (8.9cm × 8.9cm)

From Fabric C:
Cut 1 rectangle: 3½" × 4½" (8.9cm × 11.4cm)
Cut 1 rectangle: 2½" × 4½" (6.4cm × 11.4cm)
Cut 2 squares: 4½" × 4½" (11.4cm × 11.4cm)
Cut 1 rectangle: 3½" × 5½" (8.9cm × 14.0cm)
Cut 1 rectangle: 4½" × 5½" (11.4cm × 14.0cm)

From Fabric D:
Cut 1 square: 4½" × 4½" (11.4cm × 11.4cm)
Cut 2 rectangles: 4½" × 5½" (11.4cm × 14.0cm)
Cut 2 rectangles: 3½" × 4½" (8.9cm × 11.4cm)
Cut 1 rectangle: 2½" × 3½" (6.4cm × 8.9cm)

From Fabric E:
Cut 1 square: 4½" × 4½" (11.4cm × 11.4cm)
Cut 3 rectangles: 2½" × 4½" (6.4cm × 11.4cm)
Cut 2 rectangles: 3½" × 3½" (8.9cm × 8.9cm)

From Fabric F:
Cut 4 rectangles: 3½" × 4½" (8.9cm × 11.4cm)
Cut 1 rectangle: 2½" × 3½" (6.4cm × 8.9cm)
Cut 1 rectangle: 4½" × 5½" (11.4cm × 14.0cm)

From Fabric G:
Cut 1 rectangle: 2½" × 4½" (6.4cm × 11.4cm)
Cut 2 squares: 4½" × 4½" (11.4cm × 11.4cm)
Cut 1 rectangle: 3½" × 5½" (8.9cm × 14.0cm)
Cut 1 rectangle: 3½" × 4½" (8.9cm × 11.4cm)
Cut 1 rectangle: 4½" × 5½" (11.4cm × 14.0cm)

From Fabric H:
Cut 1 rectangle: 4½" × 5½" (11.4cm × 14.0cm)
Cut 2 squares: 4½" × 4½" (11.4cm × 11.4cm)
Cut 1 rectangle: 3½" × 5½" (8.9cm × 14.0cm)
Cut 1 rectangle: 3½" × 3½" (8.9cm × 8.9cm)
Cut 1 rectangle: 2½" × 4½" (6.4cm × 11.4cm)

From Ribbon A:
Cut 4 pieces: 20" (50.8cm)
Cut 2 pieces: 26" (66.0cm)

From Ribbon B:
Cut 3 pieces: 20" (50.8cm)
Cut 3 pieces: 26" (66.0cm)

1   Lay out the patchwork pieces by row according to the layout diagram (**Figure 1**).

2   Join the pieces together in row 1 using a ¼" (6mm) seam. Press the seams to the right.

3   Continue joining the patchwork pieces row by row. Press odd rows (1, 3 and 5) to the right; press even rows (2, 4 and 6) to the left.

4   Join row 1 to row 2. Press the seam down toward row 2. Continue joining rows until all the rows are joined together, pressing all seams down. Set the patchwork aside.

5   Spray the front of the foam core with spray adhesive.

6   Cover the foam core with the batting piece.

7   Pull the batting from the front of the foam core to the back. Starting at the corners, use small appliqué pins to secure the batting along the edge of the foam core, inserting a pin every 2" (5.1cm) or so.

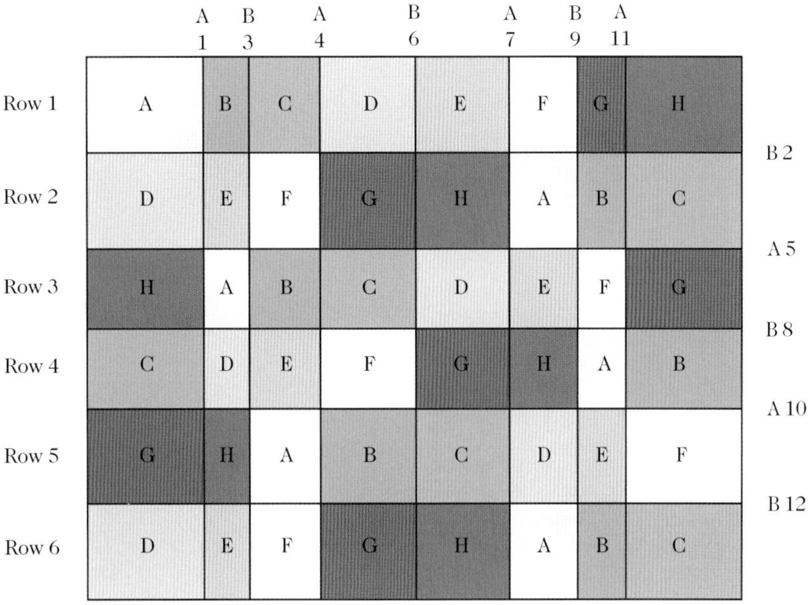

Figure 1 diagram

Top column labels: A 1, B 3, A 4, B 6, A 7, B 9, A 11

Right side labels: B 2, A 5, B 8, A 10, B 12

Row 1	A	B	C	D	E	F	G	H
Row 2	D	E	F	G	H	A	B	C
Row 3	H	A	B	C	D	E	F	G
Row 4	C	D	E	F	G	H	A	B
Row 5	G	H	A	B	C	D	E	F
Row 6	D	E	F	G	H	A	B	C

FIGURE 1

8 Once all the edges of the batting are secure, you may trim away some of the batting, leaving at least 1" (2.5cm) of batting overlapping to the back of the foam core.

9 Lay the patchwork wrong-side up. Lay the foam core onto the patchwork with the batting side down. The patchwork should extend evenly around all 4 sides by 2" (5.1cm).

10 Pull the patchwork from the front to the back. Starting at the corners, use small appliqué pins to secure the patchwork along the edge of the foam core, inserting a pin every 2" (5.1cm) or so.

11 Once all the edges of the patchwork are secure, you are ready to attach the ribbon. Following Figure 1, start with a short piece of Ribbon A. Extend the ribbon over the edge by about 1" (2.5cm) and place 1 appliqué pin along the edge of the foam core to secure the ribbon. Pull the ribbon across the patchwork to the other side and place a second pin along the edge of the foam core to secure. This end of the ribbon should also extend to the back side of the foam core by 1" (2.5cm) or more.

12 Continue pinning pieces of ribbon following the order shown in Figure 1. For the last 3 or 4 pieces of ribbon, you may choose to weave the ribbon in and out of a few of the previous pieces of ribbon. This will keep the ribbon a bit more secure.

13 Turning the piece to the wrong side, secure any loose edges of ribbon and fabric with masking tape. Use small strips of tape until all the raw edges are masked down and secure.

14 You may now frame the piece. The back of the frame will hide all the tape. If you prefer not to frame your memory board, cut a piece of felt the size of the back of the memory board. Use spray adhesive to adhere the felt to the back of the board. To hang, stitch small metal triangles (available at framing and craft stores) to the back of the board on the left and right sides. String a wire through each triangle, twisting the ends of the wire to secure.

Framed Appliqué Roses

The image of the rose has fascinated me for years. It reminds me of my paternal grandmother, Amelia. She was a great lover of roses and tended to them in her garden. My home is filled with rose imagery, much of it on things I have collected over time. I also love to appliqué them in my work. I thought it would be lovely to set a few blocks in vintage-inspired frames so I could admire them daily in my bedroom.

SUPPLIES

- Assorted scraps for appliqué
- ⅓ yard (0.3m) fabric for background
- 2 vintage or vintage-inspired frames: 8" × 10" (20.3cm × 25.4cm) each
- 2 scraps cotton batting measuring at least 8" × 10" (20.3cm × 25.4cm) each
- Hand quilting thread
- General appliqué supplies, as listed on page 8
- Patterns on pages 126–127

1   Cut each appliqué background piece to 12" × 14" (30.5cm × 35.6cm).

2   Complete the appliqué using the appliqué guidelines on pages 9–11 and the patterns on pages 126–127.

3   After the appliqué is complete, trim each rose block to 11" × 13" (27.9cm × 33.0cm).

4   Cut 1 piece of 8" × 10" (20.3cm × 25.4cm) batting for each rose block.

5   Remove the glass from 1 frame and set the frame aside.

6   Lay 1 rose block wrong-side up. Lay the batting on top of the rose block. Lay the glass on top of the batting.

7   Carefully pull the excess rose block fabric up over the glass to the back side of the piece. Turn the piece over to ensure the rose appliqué is centered on the glass.

8   Using a needle and a long piece of quilting thread, stitch from one side of the turned fabric across the glass to the opposite side of the turned fabric (**Figure 1**). With each long stitch, carefully pull the fabric taut to make it fit snugly against the glass. Complete the stitches on these first 2 sides.

9   Before stitching the remaining 2 sides, fold the corners (**Figure 2**). Then fold the fabric around the glass to create a mitered corner (**Figure 3**). You may use pins to hold the miter in place while stitching.

10   Complete the remaining 2 sides by stitching vertically across the first set of stitches. Turn the piece over occasionally to ensure the front of the piece is centered and fitting snugly against the glass.

11   Remove the pins.

12   Carefully insert the rose appliqué block into the frame. Attach the back of the frame.

13   Repeat steps 5–12 for the second rose block.

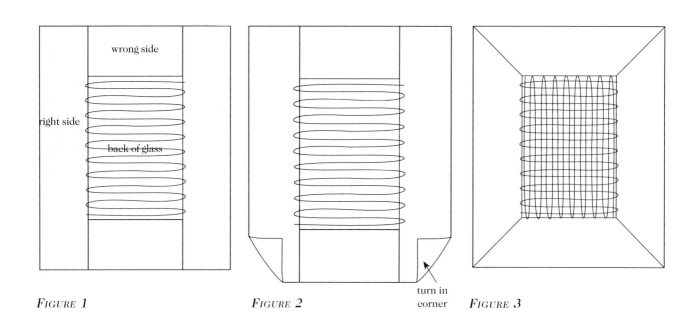

FIGURE 1   FIGURE 2   turn in corner   FIGURE 3

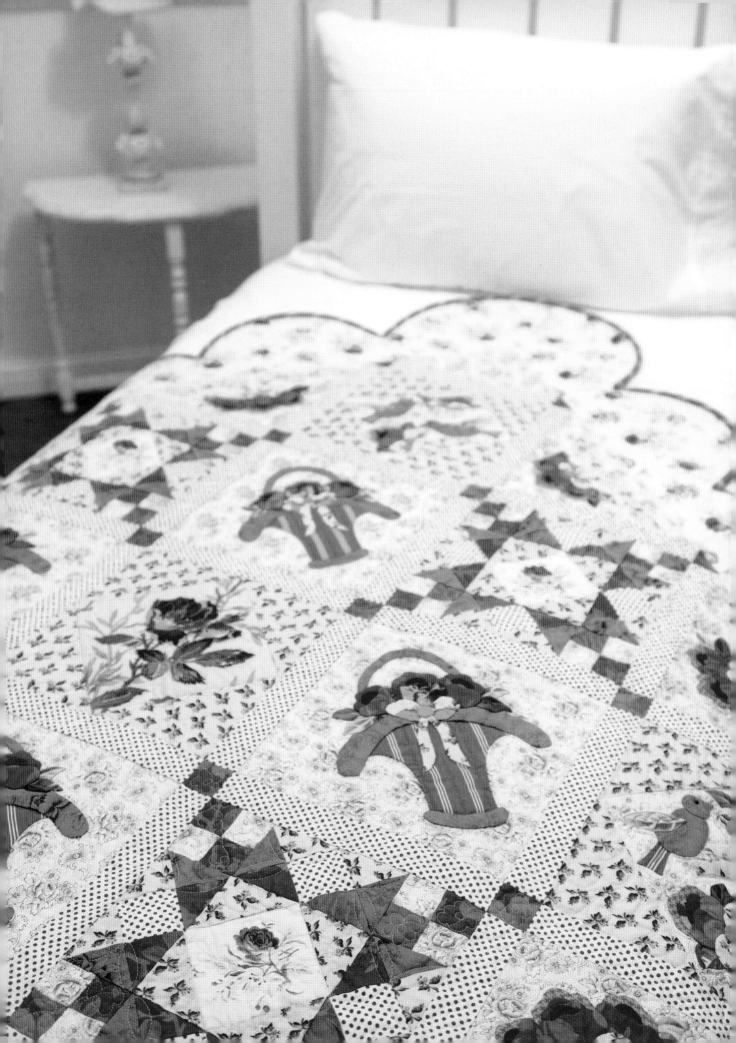

Appliqué Bed Quilt

This beautifully set quilt is the perfect blend of appliqué and patchwork. The darling basket, bird and floral motifs will add charm to any bedroom. Choose a grouping of eight fabrics and watch this heirloom come alive one block at a time. The scalloped border adds the finishing touch to this adorable design.

FINISHED SIZE

- 59" × 59" (150.0cm × 150.0cm)

SUPPLIES

- 2⅜ yards (2.2m) fabric for center of pieced block and outer border (Fabric 1)

- ⅝ yard (0.6m) fabric for pieced block and sashing (Fabric 2)

- 2⅜ yards (2.2m) fabric for appliqué backgrounds, corner triangles (Fabric 3)

- ⅝ yard (0.6m) fabric for pieced blocks, bird appliqué block corners, center block (Fabric 4)

- ⅜ yard (0.3m) fabric for pieced blocks, posts, small setting triangles (Fabric 5)

- ⅛ yard (0.1m) fabric for pieced blocks (Fabric 6)

- 9" × 9" (22.9cm × 22.9cm) fabric for center motif of center patchwork block (Fabric 7)

- 1 yard (0.9m) fabric for bias binding, basket appliqué (Fabric 8)

- 3¼ yards (3.0m) fabric for backing

- Assorted scraps or fat eighths for appliqué

- General appliqué supplies, as listed on page 8

- General patchwork supplies, as listed on page 16

- Patterns on pages 134–139

CUTTING INSTRUCTIONS

From Fabric 1:
First cut 4 strips for outer border: 10" × length of fabric (25.4cm × length of fabric)
Then cut 4 A squares: 4" × 4" (10.2cm × 10.2cm)

From Fabric 2:
Cut 16 F squares: 2¼" × 2¼" (5.7cm × 5.7cm)
Cut 36 strips for sashing: 1¾" × 10½" (4.4cm × 26.7cm)

From Fabric 3:
Cut 2 G strips: 1¾" × WOF (4.4cm × WOF)
Cut 4 squares for Basket block: 10½" × 10½" (26.7cm × 26.7cm)
Cut 4 squares for Bird block: 7½" × 7½" (19.1cm × 19.1cm)
Cut 2 squares for flower setting triangles: 15⅜" × 15⅜" (39.1cm × 39.1cm), then cut in half on both diagonals
Cut 2 squares for corner setting triangles: 8¾" × 8¾" (22.2cm × 22.2cm), then cut in half on the diagonal

From Fabric 4:
Cut 8 B squares: 3⅜" × 3⅜" (8.6cm × 8.6cm), then cut in half on one diagonal
Cut 8 E squares: 3¾" × 3¾" (9.5cm × 9.5cm), then cut in half on both diagonals
Cut 8 squares for Bird block: 6⅛" × 6⅛" (15.6cm × 15.6cm), then cut in half on one diagonal
Cut 2 squares for Center block: 6⅛" × 6⅛" (15.6cm × 15.6cm), then cut in half on one diagonal

From Fabric 5:
Cut 8 C squares: 3¾" × 3¾" (9.5cm × 9.5cm), then cut in half on both diagonals
Cut 2 H strips: 1¾" × WOF (4.4cm × WOF)
Cut 12 squares for posts: 1¾" × 1¾" (4.4cm × 4.4cm)
Cut 4 squares for small setting triangles: 3¼" × 3¼" (8.3cm × 8.3cm), then cut in half on both diagonals

From Fabric 6:
Cut 8 D squares: 3¾" × 3¾" (9.5cm × 9.5cm), then cut in half on both diagonals

From Fabric 7:
Fussy cut 1 square for Center block: 7½" × 7½" (19.1cm × 19.1cm), centering floral image

MAKING 4 PATCHWORK BLOCKS

1 Stitch 1 B triangle to 1 side of an A square. Press the seam toward the B triangle.

2 Continue adding B triangles to each side of A until all 4 have been added (**Figure 1**). This creates Unit 1.

3 Square up the block to ensure ¼" (6mm) seam allowance around all edges of the block.

4 Repeat steps 1–3 for the remaining A squares and B triangles for a total of 4 of Unit 1. Set aside.

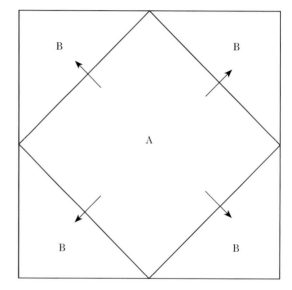

FIGURE 1

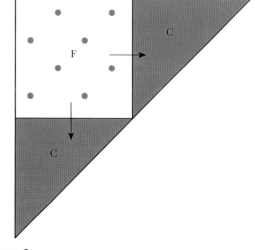

FIGURE 2

5   Join 1 C triangle to each side of 1 F square (see **Figure 2**). Press the seam toward the C triangles.

6   Square up the bottom edge of the unit to ensure exactly ¼" (6mm) seam allowance is available before joining to the next unit. This creates Unit 2.

7   Repeat steps 5–6 for a total of 16 of Unit 2.

8   Join the left side of 1 E triangle to the right side of 1 D triangle (**Figure 3**). Press the seam toward the E triangle. This creates Unit 3. Repeat for a total of 16 of Unit 3.

9   Join the left side of 1 D triangle to right side of 1 E triangle. Press the seam toward the E triangle (**Figure 4**). This creates Unit 4. Repeat for a total of 16 of Unit 4.

10 Join 1 Unit 3 to the left side of Unit 2. Press the seam toward Unit 3. Join 1 Unit 4 to the right side of Unit 2 (**Figure 5**). Press the seam toward Unit 4. This creates Unit 5.

11 Repeat step 10 for a total of 16 of Unit 5. Square each of the units before moving forward.

12 Join 1 H strip to 1 G strip. Press the seam toward the H strip. Repeat for 1 additional strip set.

13 Cut the strip sets apart every 1¾" (4.4cm) until you yield a total of 32 H/G units (**Figure 6**).

14 Join the H/G units into Four Patches. This creates Unit 6. Make a total of 16 of Unit 6.

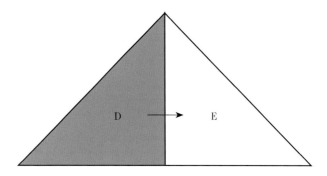

Figure 3

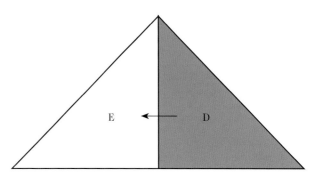

Figure 4

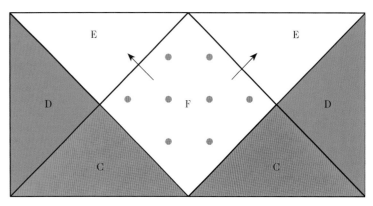

Figure 5

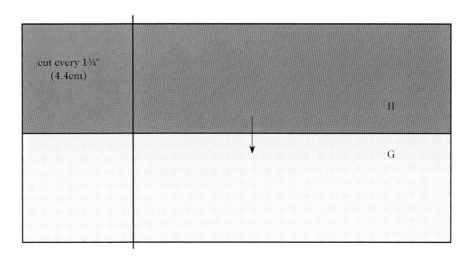

cut every 1¾" (4.4cm)

Figure 6

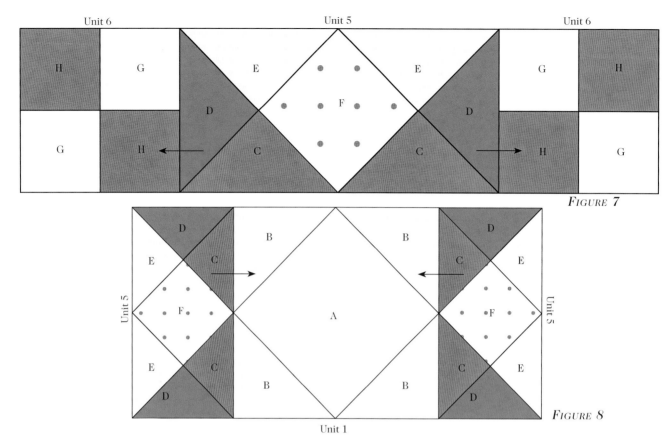

Unit 6   Unit 5   Unit 6

FIGURE 7

Unit 1

FIGURE 8

15 Join 1 Unit 6 to each side of Unit 5 (**Figure 7**). Press the seams toward Unit 6. Repeat for a total of 8. Four of these will be Row 1 of the patchwork block. The remaining 4 will be inverted to create Row 3 of the block. Set aside.

16 Join 1 Unit 5 to each side of Unit 1 (**Figure 8**). Press the seams toward Unit 1. Repeat for a total of 4. These will be Row 2 of the patchwork block.

17 Join Row 1 to Row 2. Press the seam toward Row 2. Repeat for a total of 4 Row 1/ 2 units.

18 Join Row 3 to the Row 1/ 2 unit. Press the seam toward Row 2. Repeat for a total of 4 patchwork blocks.

MAKING THE CENTER PATCHWORK BLOCK

1 Join 1 Fabric 4 triangle to each side of the Fabric 7 square. Press the seams toward the triangles. Square up the block around all 4 sides, leaving exactly ¼" (6mm) from the points out to the outer edge of the block.

MAKING 4 BIRD APPLIQUÉ BLOCKS

1 Appliqué the bird image onto a 7½" × 7½" (19.1cm × 19.1cm) Fabric 3 square using the appliqué steps described on pages 9–11.

2 Join a Fabric 4 Bird block triangle to each side of the Bird block. Press the seams toward the triangles.

3 Square up the block, leaving exactly ¼" (6mm) from the points out to the outer edge of the block.

4 Repeat steps 1–3 for the remaining 3 Bird blocks.

MAKING 4 BASKET APPLIQUÉ BLOCKS

1 Appliqué the basket image onto the 10½" × 10½" (26.7cm × 26.7cm) Fabric 3 square using the appliqué steps described on pages 9–11. Note that the basket image sits on point on the background.

2 Repeat step 1 for the remaining 3 Basket blocks.

MAKING 8 FLOWER APPLIQUÉ SETTING TRIANGLES

1 Appliqué the flower image onto a Fabric 3 flower setting triangle using the appliqué steps described on pages 9–11.

2 Repeat step 1 for the remaining 7 flower setting triangles.

JOINING THE BLOCKS INTO ROWS

1 Join the following, pressing all seams toward the sashing (**Figure 9**):
Row 1: small setting triangle, sashing, small setting triangle

2 Row 2: flower setting triangle, sashing, Bird block, sashing, flower setting triangle

3 Row 3: small setting triangle, sashing, post, sashing, post, sashing, small setting triangle

4 Row 4: flower setting triangle, sashing, Patchwork block, sashing, Basket block, sashing, Patchwork block, sashing, flower setting triangle

5 Row 5: small setting triangle, sashing, post, sashing, post, sashing, post, sashing, post, sashing, small setting triangle

6 Row 6: sashing, Bird block, sashing, Basket block, sashing, Center Patchwork block, sashing, Basket block, sashing, Bird block, sashing

7 Row 7: small setting triangle, sashing, post, sashing, post, sashing, post, sashing, post, sashing, small setting triangle

8 Row 8: flower setting triangle, sashing, Patchwork block, sashing, Basket block, sashing, Patchwork block, sashing, flower setting triangle

9 Row 9: small setting triangle, sashing, post, sashing, post, sashing, small setting triangle

10 Row 10: flower setting triangle, sashing, Bird block, sashing, flower setting triangle

11 Row 11: small setting triangle, sashing, small setting triangle

12 Join the rows together one at a time, continuing to press all seams toward the odd-numbered rows that serve as the sashing rows.

13 Join a corner triangle onto each corner of the quilt. Press the seams to the corner triangles.

14 Square up the outer edge of the quilt from point to point to ensure the quilt is square.

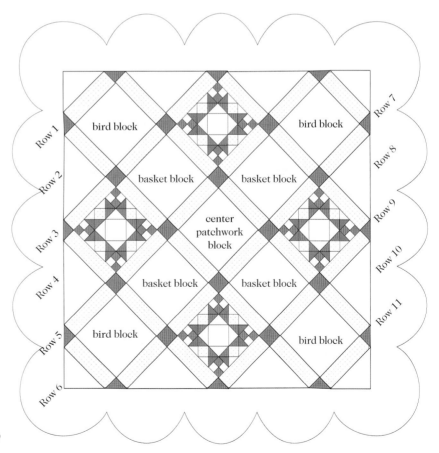

FIGURE 9

Finishing the Quilt

1 Find the midpoint of the quilt and the midpoint of a Fabric 1 border strip. Pin together and sew, starting and stopping ¼" (6mm) from each edge. Press the seam toward the border. Repeat with the 3 remaining border strips.

2 Miter each corner of the quilt at a 45° angle (see pages 52-53 for instructions). Press the seam open and trim to ¼" (6mm) seam allowance.

3 Using the templates provided on pages 137–139, trace 1 side scallop template onto freezer paper. For the corner scallop templates, fuse two pieces of freezer paper together with a small overlap to join them. Then trace the 2 corner scallop templates onto the freezer paper to create one corner scallop shape.

4 Cut the templates out with paper scissors. Iron the corner template onto 1 corner of the quilt top.

5 Mark around the edge of the freezer paper with a marking pencil. Repeat steps 4–5 and mark the other 3 corners of the quilt.

6 Find the midpoint of 1 side of the quilt and the midpoint of the side scallop template. Aligning the 2 midpoints, iron the scallop template to the quilt top. Mark around the edge of the freezer paper with a marking pencil. Repeat this step to mark the other 3 sides of the quilt.

7 Once all corners and midpoint side scallops have been marked, mark the remaining scallops on the quilt top.

8 Layer, baste and quilt as desired. To make binding easier, be sure to quilt well into the scallop area. Once the quilting is complete, cut around the marked scallops using scissors.

9 Cut the binding strips on the bias. To do this, fold the lower left corner of your binding fabric up to align with the top edge of the fabric. Align the folded edge along a horizontal line on a cutting mat. Square up one edge of the fabric to form a triangle and cut several 2⅜" (6.0cm) wide binding strips. You will need a total of 300" (7.6m) of binding.

10 Join the binding strips on the diagonal (see instructions on page 38) and press the seams open.

11 Starting on a curve, attach the binding to the front of the quilt. It is best to pin 1 scallop and stitch it, then break the thread when you reach each V. Pin and stitch the next scallop, and continue until the entire binding is attached.

12 Once the entire binding is attached, fold the binding to the back side of the quilt and stitch down by hand.

Patterns

You may photocopy the patterns in this book to make the projects for your personal use or to give as gifts. Enlarge the patterns as necessary, as instructed in the pattern caption.

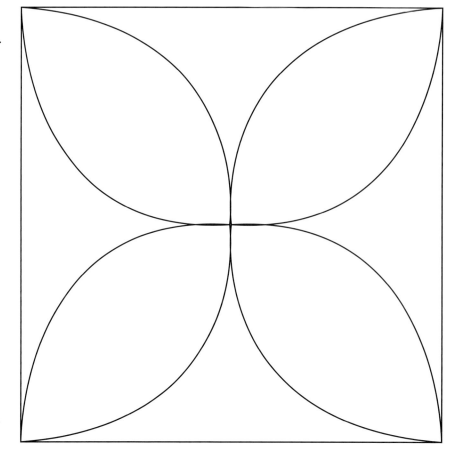

Dream

Embroidery for Artist Journal Cover, page 82. Shown here at 100%.

Petal for flower on Flower Apron, page 28. Shown here at 100%.

Leaf appliqué for Tablecloth Quilt, page 34. Shown here at 100%.

Add a small bead
for the eyes.

Stem stitch 2
strands of floss.

Chain stitch the rope
using 2 strands of floss.

*Appliqué for Artist Journal Cover,
page 82. Shown here at 100%.*

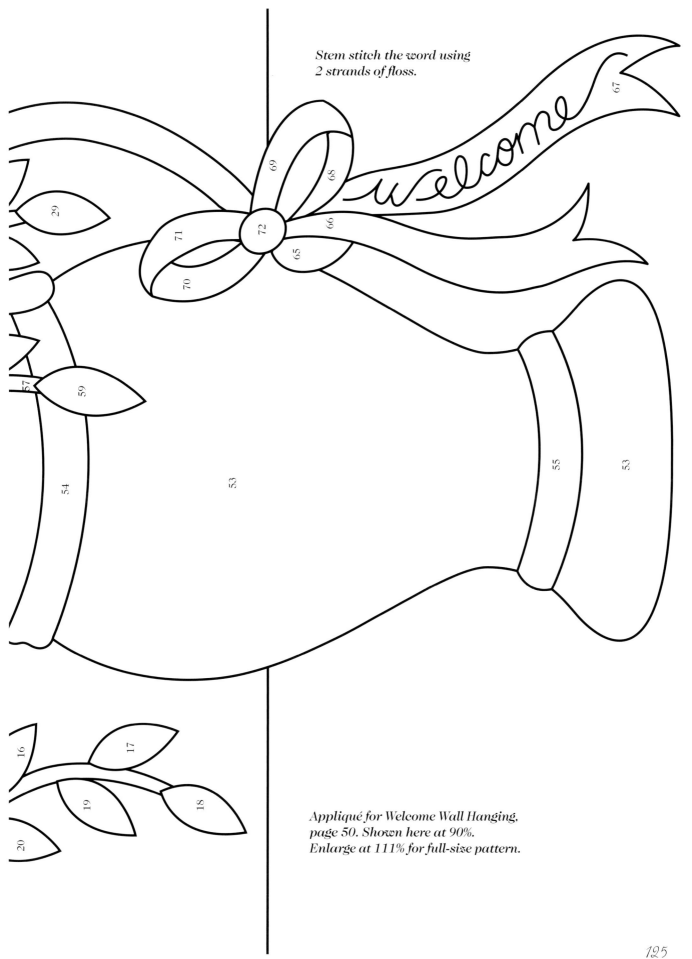

Stem stitch the word using
2 strands of floss.

Appliqué for Welcome Wall Hanging,
page 50. Shown here at 90%.
Enlarge at 111% for full-size pattern.

Appliqué for Framed Appliqué Roses,
page 113. Shown here at 100%.

Appliqué for Framed Appliqué Roses, page 110. Shown here at 100%.

*Stem stitch the veins
using 2 strands of floss.*

*Appliqué for Appliqué Dish
Towels, page 24. Shown here at
100%.*

*Reverse appliqué for Fabric
Coasters, page 90. Shown here
at 100%.*

French knot the
flower centers using
2 strands of floss.

Stem stitch the veins
using 2 strands of floss.

Appliqué for Appliqué Dish
Towels, page 24. Shown here at
100%.

LAUNDRY

Embroidery for Laundry Bag,
page 60. Shown here at 100%.

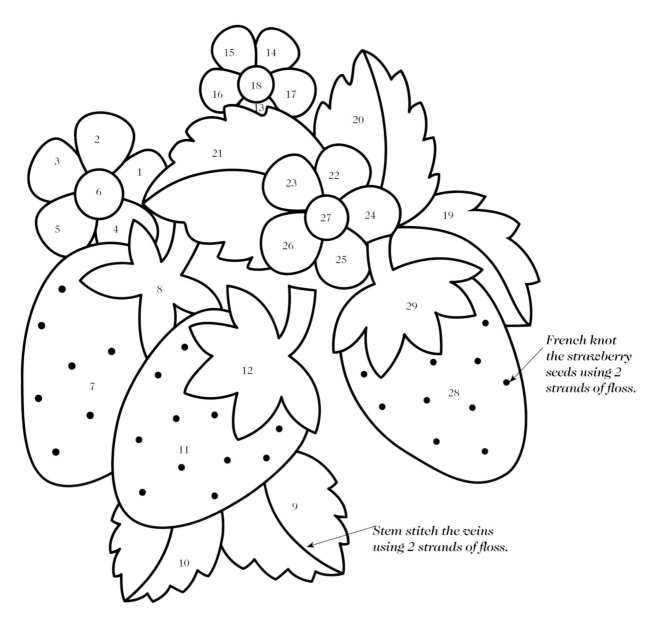

French knot
the strawberry
seeds using 2
strands of floss.

Stem stitch the veins
using 2 strands of floss.

Appliqué for Appliqué Dish
Towels, page 24. Shown here at
100%.

Embroidery for Pedestal
Pincushion, page 86. Shown
here at 100%.

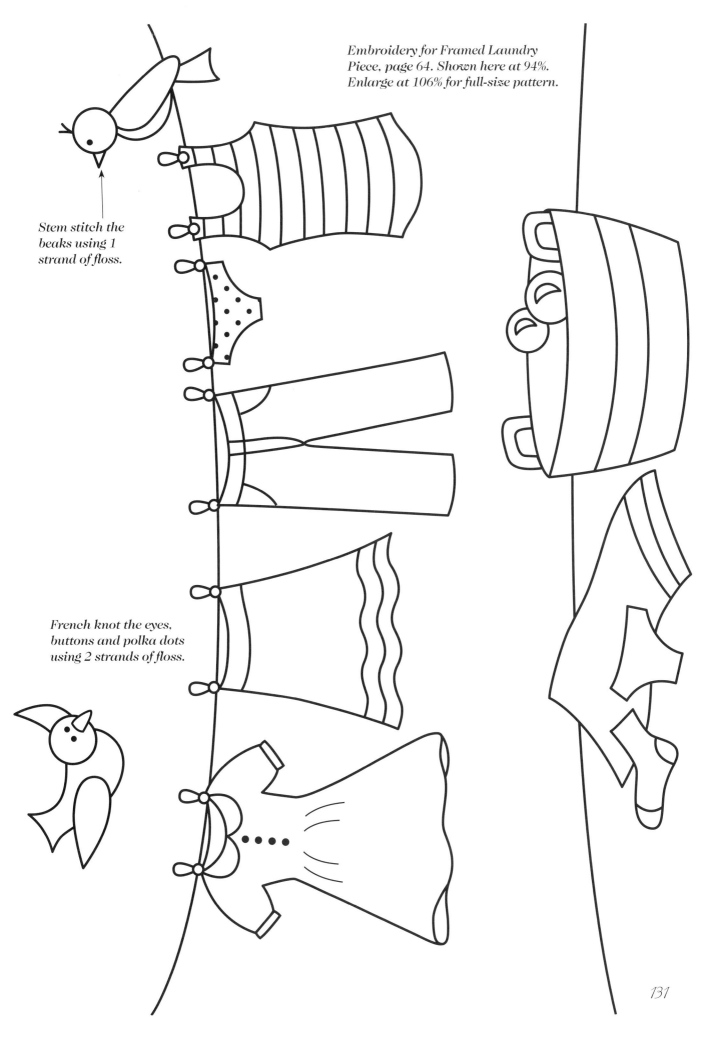

Embroidery for Framed Laundry
Piece, page 64. Shown here at 94%.
Enlarge at 106% for full-size pattern.

Stem stitch the
beaks using 1
strand of floss.

French knot the eyes,
buttons and polka dots
using 2 strands of floss.

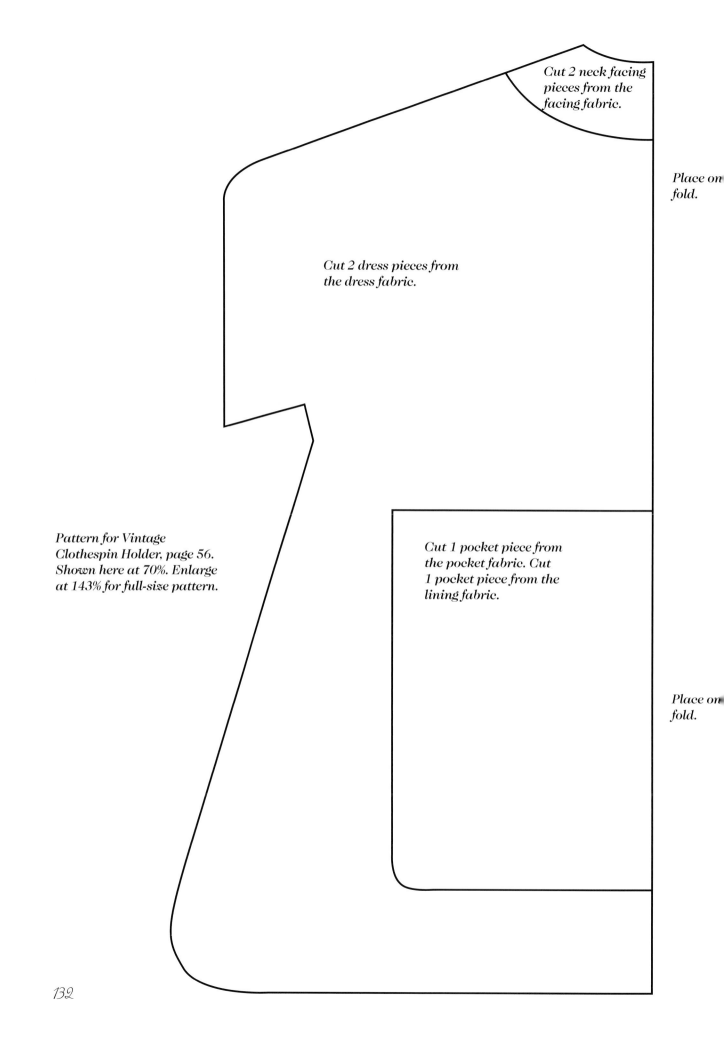

Cut 2 neck facing
pieces from the
facing fabric.

Place on
fold.

Cut 2 dress pieces from
the dress fabric.

Cut 1 pocket piece from
the pocket fabric. Cut
1 pocket piece from the
lining fabric.

Place on
fold.

Pattern for Vintage
Clothespin Holder, page 56.
Shown here at 70%. Enlarge
at 143% for full-size pattern.

Stem stitch the hanger using 2 strands of floss.

Stem stitch the border using 2 strands of floss.

5

5

2

3

4

6

French knot the dots with 2 strands of floss.

Stem stitch the tie using 2 strands of floss.

1

4

13

14

12

15

9

19

8

18

17

7

16

10

11

Stem stitch the branch using 2 strands of floss.

Appliqué for Mini Appliqué Vignette, page 76. Shown here at 90%. Enlarge at 111% for full-size pattern.

Appliqué for Appliqué Bed Quilt, page 114. Shown here at 100%.

Appliqué for Appliqué Bed Quilt, page 114. Shown here at 100%.

Appliqué for Appliqué Bed Quilt, page 114. Shown here at 100%.

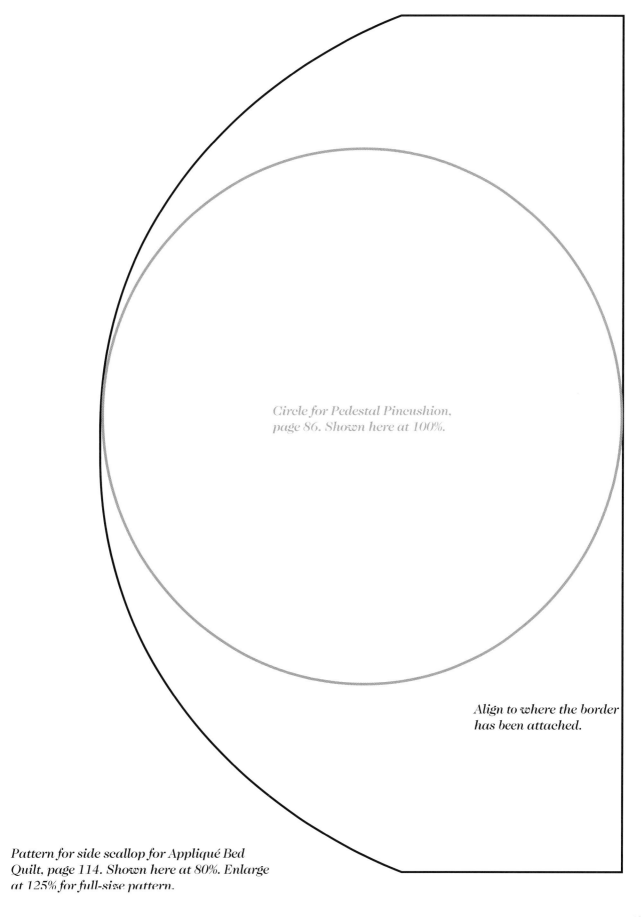

Circle for Pedestal Pincushion,
page 86. Shown here at 100%.

Align to where the border
has been attached.

Pattern for side scallop for Appliqué Bed
Quilt, page 114. Shown here at 80%. Enlarge
at 125% for full-size pattern.

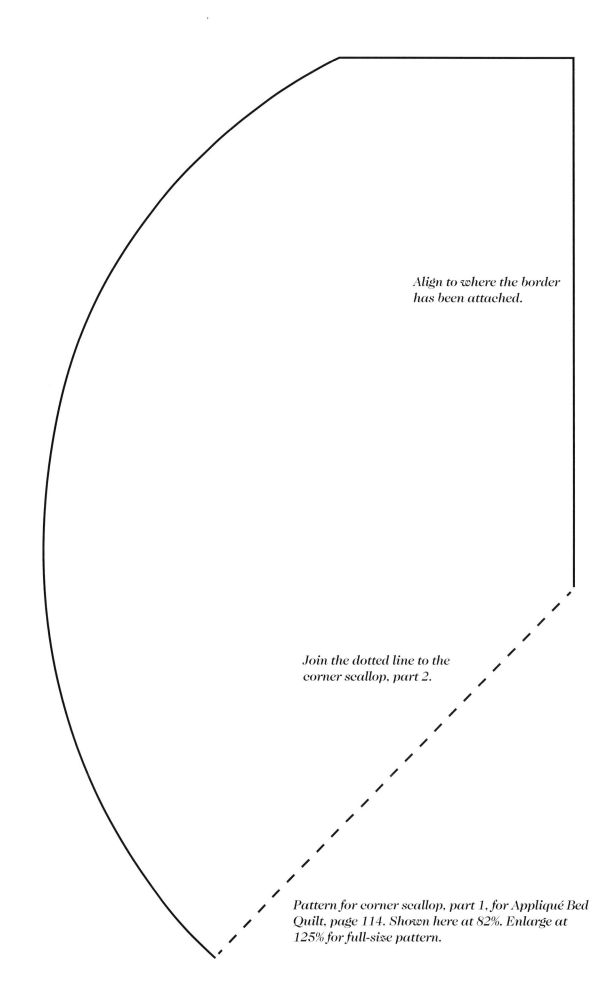

Align to where the border
has been attached.

Join the dotted line to the
corner scallop, part 2.

Pattern for corner scallop, part 1, for Appliqué Bed
Quilt, page 114. Shown here at 82%. Enlarge at
125% for full-size pattern.

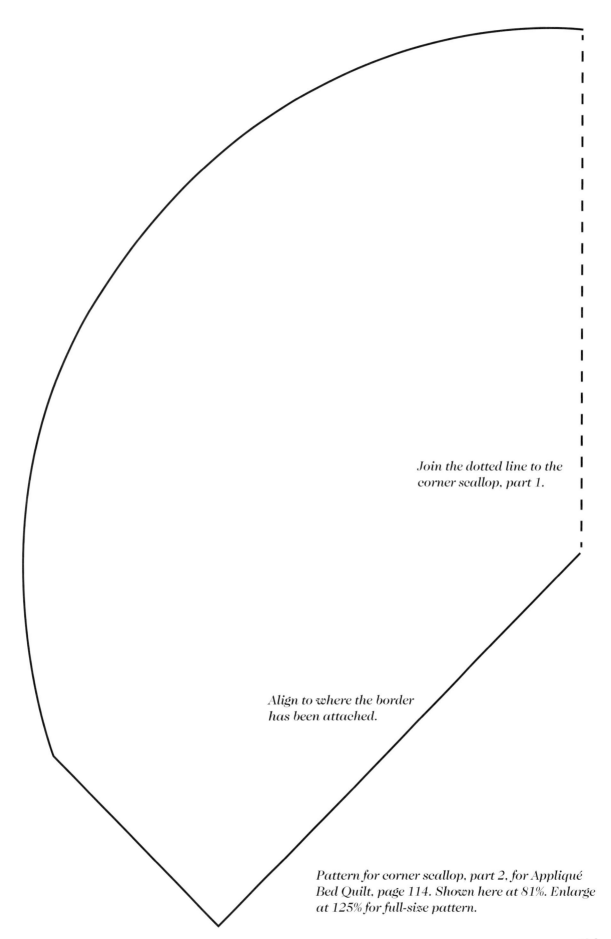

Join the dotted line to the corner scallop, part 1.

Align to where the border has been attached.

Pattern for corner scallop, part 2, for Appliqué Bed Quilt, page 114. Shown here at 81%. Enlarge at 125% for full-size pattern.

Resources

Products used to create the projects in this book were made by the following manufacturers. Look for these products at your local fabric or craft store, or contact the manufacturer for retailer information.

Coats & Clark
Anchor embroidery floss
800-648-1479
http://www.coatsandclark.com

DMC
Machine embroidery thread
973-589-0606
http://www.dmc-usa.com

C. Jenkins Company
Freezer paper
www.cjenkinscompany.com

Foxglove Cottage
Jeana Kimball ¾" appliqué pins, Jeana
Kimball #9 embroidery needles, Jeana
Kimball #10 straw needles
435-462-9618
www.jeanakimballquilter.com

Westminster Fibers
Verna Mosquera's fabric collections for
FreeSpirit Fabrics and FreeSpirit Basics
Fabrics
866-907-3305
www.freespiritfabric.com

Westminster Fibers Fabrics
800-445-9276
info@westminsterfibers.com
In the UK, Coats Crafts
+44 (0) 1484 681881
consumer.ccuk@coats.com

In the rest of Europe, Coats GMBH
+49 (0)7162 14-208
irmgard.paffrath@coats.com
Antiques and Photo Props
A special thanks to the local antique
stores that always stock their shelves
with wonderful vintage treasures.
Many of my finds from these shops are
featured in the photographs in this book.

American Harvest
438 Main Street
Pleasanton, CA 94566
925-485-1577
www.americanharvestinc.com

Cottage Jewel
100 West Prospect Avenue
Danville, CA 94526
925-837-2664
www.cottagejewel.com

Gardenseed
352 Hartz Avenue
Danville, CA 94526
925-838-6481
www.gardenseed.danville.com

Index

Acknowledgments

This book has been a dream for some time. It was long in the making—first in my mind, then on paper and finally in the form of sewn treasures made lovingly by hand. I am incredibly grateful for the opportunity to share my artistic vision with the world. To those who have wished me well and embraced my designs, I thank you for your support and hope to inspire you once again.

To my extremely patient husband, Miguel, for your love and support of my need to be creative on a daily basis; and to my two extraordinary sons, Milo and Nico, for always understanding when Mommy needs to work. I love you all so much!

To my mom and dad. Everyone should have the gift of parents as inspiring and loving as mine. You taught me to always work hard, approach life with passion and follow my dreams. I am forever grateful for all you have blessed me with.

To Omar, Lisa, Luke, Marco and Ellie. I am so very lucky to call you family and to have you in my life.

To my close friends, for your willingness to always listen and for understanding how incredibly busy my life can be.

To my dear friend, Pam Stipic, for your wonderful dedication to the Vintage Spool, for your amazing organizational skills and for always keeping me grounded.

To the sweetest woman I know, JoAnn Carpenter, for your wonderful quilting, for always greeting me with a smile and for your endless hours spent getting my projects done in a hurry.

To my treasured friend, Brooke Shay, for your friendship and the energy you bring to the Vintage Spool. I so look forward to what lies ahead.

To my Tuesday night quilting buddies, thank you for letting me be myself. You always supply an evening of laughs and friendship. I truly look forward to both week after week.

To my sewing ladies, Wilma Lawrence, Heidi Gorthy, Jean Maher, Marsha Smith, Bobbie Ball, Mauna Wagner and Karen Anderson, for your wonderful willingness to always help stitch samples and for your amazingly beautiful appliqué work.

To all my past students and followers of my designs. Thank you for your incredible support over the years. My creative juices keep flowing knowing you are out there waiting for more.

To Gregory Case, for your wonderful photography, for your incredible patience and for always going the extra mile to get it just right.

To the whole team at Westminster Fibers who, from start to finish, help to create gorgeous fabrics. They have a beautiful hand and are wonderful to work with. You help to perfect every collection.

To Coats & Clark for the generous supply of lovely Anchor floss for the embroidery portion of this book.

To everyone at F+W Media and David & Charles for all of your hard work. Thank you for your patience with this first-time author. It has been a wonderful learning experience.

About the Author

Other fine David & Charles books are available from your favorite bookstore, fabric store or online supplier.
email: postmaster@davidandcharles.co.uk

www.fwmedia.com

17 16 15 14 13   5 4 3 2 1

Distributed in Canada by Fraser Direct
100 Armstrong Avenue
Georgetown, ON, Canada L7G 5S4
Tel: (905) 877-4411

Distributed in the U.K. and Europe
by F&W Media International
LTD Brunel House, Forde Close, Newton Abbot, TQ12 4PU, UK
Tel: (+44) 1626 323200, Fax: (+44) 1626 323319
Email: enquiries@fwmedia.com

Distributed in Australia by Capricorn Link
P.O. Box 704, S. Windsor NSW, 2756 Australia
Tel: (02) 4560-1600   Fax: (02) 4577-5288
email: books@capricornlink.com.au

SRN: W8867
ISBN-13: 978-1-4402-3042-4
ISBN-10: 1-4402-3042-0

Edited by Christine Doyle
Designed by Charly Bailey
Photography by Gregory Case
Illustrated by Kendra-Louise Lapolla
Production coordinated by Greg Nock

Verna Mosquera's appliqué technique is industry-renowned and is just one of the special features of her vintage, romantic designs that make them unique, current and instantly recognizable as hers. In 2004, Verna launched her pattern design business, The Vintage Spool. Since then, The Vintage Spool's designs have earned international acclaim, and the company currently distributes more than forty-five designs worldwide. Verna also designs fabric for FreeSpirit and has had eight collections with them.

METRIC CONVERSION CHART

CONVERT	TO	MULTIPLY BY
Inches	Centimeters	2.54
Centimeters	Inches	0.4
Feet	Centimeters	30.5
Centimeters	Feet	0.03
Yards	Meters	0.9
Meters	Yards	1.1

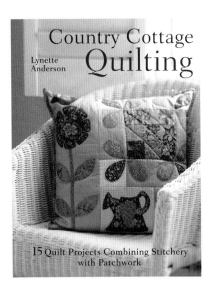

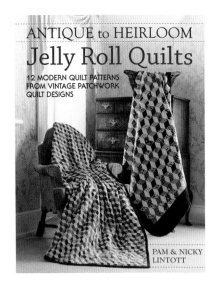

Fresh from the Clothesline
Quilts and Small Projects with Vintage Appeal
by Darlene Zimmerman

Twenty-two fantastic quilting and sewing projects are brought to you in Fresh From The Clothesline! You'll find a fun range of projects from quick-to-sew items to large-and-loving-them quilts, all featuring beautiful 1930s reproduction fabrics. Enjoy the easy-to-follow instructions and crisp illustrations, as well as the yummy recipes and entertaining stories featured alongside the projects.

ISBN-13: 978-1-4402-1775-3

Country Cottage Quilting
15 Quilt Projects Combining Stitchery with Patchwork
by Lynette Anderson

Lynette Anderson's country cottage garden provides the inspiration for this collection of fifteen gorgeous projects to create. This book includes wall quilts, everyday bags and sumptuous cushion covers, all in Lynette's distinctive country style. These stunning designs combine charming hand embroidery with traditional patchwork and quilting techniques for you to create and enjoy.

ISBN-13: 978-1-4463-0039-8

Antique to Heirloom Jelly Roll Quilts
12 Modern Quilt Patterns from Vintage Patchwork Quilt Designs
by Pam & Nicky Lintott

Pam and Nicky Lintott bring you twelve new Jelly Roll quilt designs. Each clever quilt pattern uses just one Jelly Roll and has been designed to make the best use of your fabric while preserving the vintage style of each antique patchwork quilt. Detailed step-by-step instructions, full-color diagrams and beautiful photographs make this book a must have.

ISBN: 978-1-4463-0182-1

Find more inspiration for your creative lifestyle at sewdaily.com